DAVID MALOUF

David Malouf was born in Brisbane in 1934. He is the author of ten works of fiction, including *Johnno*, *An Imaginary Life, Fly Away Peter, The Great World* and *Remembering Babylon*. His latest novel is *Conversation at Curlew Creek*. He is also a poet and a librettist. His work has been translated into most European languages, and into Arabic and Chinese. *The Great World* won the Miles Franklin Award, the Commonwealth Prize for Fiction, and the Prix Femina Etranger. *Remembering Babylon* was shortlisted for the Booker Prize, and won the *Los Angeles Times* Prize for Fiction and the inaugural International IMPAC Dublin Literary Award.

BOYER LECTURES

Each year the ABC invites a prominent Australian to present the result of his or her work and thinking on major social, scientific or cultural issues in a series of radio talks known as the Boyer Lectures. The series was inaugurated in 1959 under the title ABC Lectures but in 1961 was renamed as a memorial to the late Sir Richard Boyer who, as chairman of the ABC, had been one of those responsible for its introduction.

a spirit of play

The making of Australian consciousness

David **Malouf**

Dec '98

For Garry & Teri,

We're enjoying playing and sharing our understandings with you.

Much love, Jossie & Ken

Adelaide SA.

ABC
BOOKS

For kind permission to quote from the following, the author and publishers would like to thank:

ETT Imprint for Mary Gilmore, 'Old Botany Bay' from *Selected Poems*, ETT Imprint, Sydney, 1998.
HarperCollins Publishers for Kenneth Slessor, 'South Country' from *Selected Poems*.

Published by ABC Books for the
AUSTRALIAN BROADCASTING CORPORATION
GPO Box 9994 Sydney NSW 2001

First published 1998

National Library of Australia
Cataloguing-in-Publication entry
Malouf, David, 1934– .
   A spirit of play.
   ISBN 0 7333 0726 4.
   1. Social change – Australia. 2. Social evolution –
   Australia. 3. Australia – Social life and customs. 4.
   Australia – History. I. Australian Broadcasting
   Corporation. II. Title. (Series : Boyer lectures ; 1998).
303.40994.

Cover designed by Reno Design Group
Set in Lingwood 12/16.5 pt by
Midland Typesetters, Maryborough, Victoria
Printed and bound in Australia by
Australian Print Group, Maryborough, Victoria

5 4 3 2 1

Contents

The Island

Looking down the long line of coast this morning as I begin these lectures, I see the first rays of the sun strike Mount Warning and am aware, as the light floods west, what a distance it is to the far side of our country—two time zones and more than three thousand kilometres away, yet how easily the whole landmass sits in my head—as an island or, as I sometimes think of it, a raft we have all scrambled aboard, a new float of lives in busy interaction, of assembly lines and highways, of ideals given body as executives and courts, of routine housekeeping arrangements and objects in passage from hand to hand. To comprehend the thing in all its action and variety and contradiction is a task for the imagination, yet this morning, as always, it is simple there, substantial and ordinary.

When Europeans first came to these shores one of the things they brought with them, as a kind of gift to the land itself, was something that could never have existed before: a vision of the continent in its true form as an island that was not just a way of seeing it, and seeing it whole, but of seeing how it fitted into the rest of the world. And this seems to have happened even before circumnavigation established that it actually was an island. No group of Aboriginal Australians, however ancient and deep their understanding of the land, can ever have seen the place in just this way. It has made a difference. If Aborigines are a land-dreaming people, what we latecomers share is a sea-dreaming, to which the image of Australia as an island has from the beginning been central.

This is hardly surprising. Sydney, in its early days, was first and foremost a seaport; all its dealings were with the sea. Our earliest productive industries were not wheat-growing or sheep-raising but whaling and sealing. It took us nearly 30 years to cross the first land barrier. Right up to the end of the nineteenth century our settlements were linked by coastal steamer, not by road or rail. In his sonnet 'Australia', Bernard O'Dowd speaks of Australia's 'virgin helpmate, Ocean', as if the island continent were mystically married to its surrounding ocean as Venice was to the Adriatic.

As the off-shoot of a great naval power we felt at home with the sea. It was an element over which we had control; more, certainly, than we had at the beginning over the land. It was what we looked to for all our comings and goings, for all that was new—for news. And this sense of being at home with the sea made distances that might otherwise have been unimaginable seem shorter. It brought Britain and Europe closer than 10,000 miles on the globe might have suggested, and kept us tethered, for longer than we might otherwise have been, by sea-routes whose ports of call in the days before air travel constituted a litany of connection that every child of my generation knew by heart. Distance is not always a matter of miles. Measured in feelings it can redefine itself as closeness.

And this notion of an island continent, contained and containable, had other consequences.

Most nations establish themselves through a long series of border conflicts with neighbours. This is often the major thrust of their history. Think of the various wars between Germany and France, or Russia and Poland, or of British history before the Union of the Crowns.

Australia's borders were a gift of nature. We did not

have to fight for them. In our case, history and geography coincided, and we soon hit upon the idea that the single continent must one day be a single nation. What this means is that all our wars of conquest, all our sources of conflict, have been internal. Conquest of space to begin with, in a series of daring explorations of the *land*, which were also acts of possession different from the one that made it ours merely in law. This was possession in the form of knowledge by naming and mapping, by taking its spaces into our heads, and at last into our imagination and consciousness. Conquest of every form of internal division and difference: conquest of the original possessors, for example, in a war more extensive than we have wanted to recognise. Later, there was the attempted resolution, through an act of Federation, of the fraternal division between the states; and, longer lasting and less amenable of solution, of the conflict, once Federation had been achieved, between the states and the Federal Government. Also, more darkly, suppression, in acts of law-making and social pressure and through subtle forms of exclusion, of all those whom we have, at one time or another, declared to be outsiders among us, and in their various ways alien, even when they were Australians like the rest. That early vision of wholeness produced a corresponding anxiety, the fear of fragmentation, and for too long the only answer we had to it was the imposition of a deadening conformity.

In time, the vision of the continent as whole and unique in its separation from the rest of the world produced the idea that it should be *kept* separate, that only in isolation could its uniqueness—and ours—be preserved.

Many of the ideas that have shaped our life here, and many of the themes on which our history has been argued, settle around these notions of isolation and containment, of wholeness and the fear of fragmentation. But isolation can lead to stagnation as well as concentrated richness, and wholeness does not necessarily mean uniformity, though that is how we have generally taken it. Nor does diversity always lead to fragmentation.

As for the gift of those natural, indisputable borders, that too had a cost. It burdened us with the duty of defending them, and the fear, almost from the beginning, that they may not, in fact, be defendable.

Our first settlements outside Sydney, at Hobart in 1804 and Perth in the 1820s, were made to forestall the possibility of French occupation (and it seems Napoleon did plan a diversionary invasion for 1804). Then, at the time of the Crimean War, it was the Russians we had to keep an eye on. The Russian fleet was just seven days sailing away at Vladivostok. And then, from the beginning of this century, the Japanese. This fear of *actual* invaders, of being unable to defend our borders, led to a fear of other and less tangible forms of invasion. By people, 'lesser breeds without the Law',[1] who might sully the purity of our stock; by alien forms of culture that might prejudice our attempt to be uniquely ourselves; by ideas, and all those other forms of influence, out there in the world beyond our coast, that might undermine our morals or in various other ways divide and unsettle us. All this has made little-islanders of us; has made us decide, from time to time, to close ourselves off from influence and change, and by settling in behind our ocean wall, freeze and stop what has been from the beginning, and continues to be, a unique and exciting experiment.

■　■　■

Australia began as an experiment in human engineering. We should not allow the brutalities of the age in which it took place to obscure the fact that among the many mixed motives for the founding of the colony there were some that were progressive and idealistic. The eighteenth century was as troubled as we are by the nature of criminality and, in dealing with it, the need to balance deterrence, or as they would have called it, terror, with the opportunity to reform. Botany Bay was not just a dumping ground for unwanted criminals. It was also an experiment in reformation, in using the rejects of one society to create another.

What seems astonishing when we look about at the

world we live in here, this clean and orderly place with its high level of affluence and ease, its concern for rights and every sort of freedom, these cities in which a high level of civility is simply taken for granted and barely remarked upon, is that it should have emerged from a world that was at the beginning so *un*-free, so brutal and disorderly. It did so because these rejects of society, of whom so little might have been expected, *made* it happen. Out of their insistence that they were not to be so easily written off.

Charles Darwin, who was not always a sympathetic observer of the Australian scene, has two things to tell us of the colony as he first saw it in 1836, not quite 50 years from the beginning. 'Here', he writes in his *Journal of the Voyage of the HMS* Beagle, 'in less promising country, scores of years have affected many times more than the same number of centuries has done in South America.' That is a tribute to the pace of development in Australia, and also, no doubt, to British efficiency and moral fibre as opposed to Spanish and Portuguese fecklessness. But he has something else to say as well. 'As a means', he tells us, 'of making men honest—of converting vagabonds the most useless in one hemisphere into active citizens in another, and giving birth to a new and splendid country—and a grand centre of civilisation—it has succeeded to a degree perhaps unparalleled in history.'

When we think of our beginning, we are inclined to emphasise what is sensational in it, the many horrors, and this is understandable.[2] They were real, and indignation at injustice does credit to us—so does a passionate sympathy for its victims. Fellow-feeling for the weak and for those who fail, out of bad luck or bad judgment or ordinary human hopelessness, is one of our strongest national characteristics and has its beginning here. Our attitude to welfare, for instance, and to those who need it, is very different from the way these things are seen in some other places.

But victims, and sensational brutality and misery, are easy to imagine and identify with. What is harder to think our way into is ordinariness, the day-to-day routine of lives that, however brutal they may have been by our standards, were unremarkable except in the astonishing capacity of those who lived them (and we need to think hard about what this must have meant to individual men and women) to endure, but even more, to change; to take hold of their lives and remake themselves in terms of the opportunities offered by a second chance in a new place.

Eighteenth-century playwrights and novelists often made a criminal—a highwayman or confidence trickster or thief—their hero. Gay's *Beggar's Opera*, Defoe's *Colonel Jack* and *Captain Singleton*, Fielding's *Mr Jonathan Wild*, all play with the interesting and subversive notion that the qualities that go to the making of a successful criminal—entrepreneurial egotism, an eye for the main chance and for the weakness of others—may be the same qualities that in other circumstances make a politician or businessman. Botany Bay in some ways put this cheeky proposition to the proof.

John Locke claimed that men join a civil society or commonwealth 'for mutual protection of their lives, liberty and estates, which I call', he says 'by the general name of property'.[3] Now, if it is the need to protect property that makes men join together and become citizens, mightn't it be possible to make citizens out of vagabonds, as Darwin calls them, by *giving* them property, that is, land, but in a place so far off that they would not be tempted to return; a place where possession of property would lead them to *settle*, even when their term of exile was up? Land, that real yet mystical commodity of measured dirt that can raise a man, or a woman, from a mere nothing to an individual of status and power, and eventually, since this is what land usually ensured in the days before universal suffrage, the right to vote and have a voice in the making of the laws.

It was the promise of land, 50 acres for a man, 30 more for his wife, and 30 for each child, that was the new element in this experiment and a defining one in our history, not least because of the conflict it involved with the original owners. That is another story, another and darker history interwoven with our more triumphal one, and the conflict over land that is at the centre of it is not just about occupation and ownership; it is also about what land means. For Aboriginal people land is the foundation of spiritual being. For Europeans it represents security and status, or it is a source of wealth. The desire of ordinary men and women to become property owners was the making of this country. To own a piece of Australia, even if it was only a quarter-acre block, became the Australian dream. The desperation that lay behind it, the determination of poor men and women to grasp what was offered and raise themselves out of a landless poverty into a new class, was the source of a materialism that is still one of our most obvious characteristics. It has taken us 200 years to see that there might be another and more inward way of possessing a place, and that in this, as in so much else, the people we dispossessed had been there before us. But the fact is that for those convicts who did succeed, all this was a fairy tale come true. Samuel Terry, for instance, was transported in 1801 for stealing 400 pairs of stockings; he seems always to have done things on a large scale. He served his 7 years, and when he died in 1838 owned 19,000 acres, more than the greatest lord in England.

Of course, opportunity, however great, was also limited. Not everyone ended up as a merchant prince. But when all the savageries have been taken into account, and the disruption and pain of leaving loved ones, and a life, however unsettled, that in their mind, in their hearts too, was home, transportation worked for most of these men and women. To suggest otherwise is to deny the extent to which so many of them *did* change and become the active citizens who made our world. And there must have been some among them, like Simeon Lord and Mary Reibey or Esther Abrahams, for whom Botany Bay was not just the underside of the world but the realisation of that dream of radical English thinkers in the seventeenth century, the world turned upside down.[4] Esther Abrahams, who was transported in the First Fleet for theft, set up with, and later married, Major George Johnston, and was, for a time, the First Lady of the colony. It is Mary Gilmore who has given us our most memorable statement of all this. The old convict in her poem 'Old Botany Bay' gives a voice to many thousands who have no other voice in our history.

> I'm old
> Botany Bay;
> Stiff in the joints,
> Little to say.
>
> I am he
> Who paved the way
> That you might walk
> At your ease today.

I was the conscript
Sent to hell
To make in the desert
The living well

I bore the heat,
I blazed the track—
Furrowed and bloody
Upon my back.

I split the rock;
I felled the tree;
The nation was—
Because of me!

Old Botany Bay
Taking the sun
From day to day ...
Shame on the mouth

That would deny
The knotted hands
That set us high!

I would want to add that it wasn't just muscle and
dumb endurance that these people brought, and which
we enjoy the fruits of, but also native wit, inventiveness,

The Island*

imagination and, most of all, the amazing human capacity to re-imagine and remake themselves.

■ ■ ■

One surprising detail leaps out of the various accounts we have of the First Fleet voyage. It is this: on the night of 2 January 1788, some of the convicts on one of the ships, the *Scarborough*, as their contribution to the possibilities of diversion and simple enjoyment in the place they were coming to—and in defiance it seems, of the misery of cramped conditions and whatever terror they may have felt at their imminent arrival on a fatal shore—got up a dramatic entertainment, some sort of play.

So, smuggled in on one of those eleven little ships, along with their cargo of criminal rejects and all the necessary objects for settling a new place—the handsaws and framesaws, and the steel spade and iron shovel and three hoes and an axe and tomahawk for each man, and the woollen drawers and worsted stockings for the men, and linsey-woolsey petticoats and caps for the women, and Lieutenant George Worgan's piano,[5] and the rights and obligations that, in being argued back and forth between authority and its many subjects, would make the new place they were coming to so different from the one they left—was this spirit of make-believe, of theatre, of

The Island

The Island

imagination and, most of all, the amazing human capacity to re-imagine and remake themselves.

■ ■ ■

One surprising detail leaps out of the various accounts we have of the First Fleet voyage. It is this: on the night of 2 January 1788, some of the convicts on one of the ships, the *Scarborough*, as their contribution to the possibilities of diversion and simple enjoyment in the place they were coming to—and in defiance it seems, of the misery of cramped conditions and whatever terror they may have felt at their imminent arrival on a fatal shore—got up a dramatic entertainment, some sort of play.

So, smuggled in on one of those eleven little ships, along with their cargo of criminal rejects and all the necessary objects for settling a new place—the handsaws and framesaws, and the steel spade and iron shovel and three hoes and an axe and tomahawk for each man, and the woollen drawers and worsted stockings for the men, and linsey-woolsey petticoats and caps for the women, and Lieutenant George Worgan's piano,[5] and the rights and obligations that, in being argued back and forth between authority and its many subjects, would make the new place they were coming to so different from the one they left—was this spirit of make-believe, of theatre, of

The Island

imagination and, most of all, the amazing human capacity to re-imagine and remake themselves.

■ ■ ■

One surprising detail leaps out of the various accounts we have of the First Fleet voyage. It is this: on the night of 2 January 1788, some of the convicts on one of the ships, the *Scarborough*, as their contribution to the possibilities of diversion and simple enjoyment in the place they were coming to—and in defiance it seems, of the misery of cramped conditions and whatever terror they may have felt at their imminent arrival on a fatal shore—got up a dramatic entertainment, some sort of play.

So, smuggled in on one of those eleven little ships, along with their cargo of criminal rejects and all the necessary objects for settling a new place—the handsaws and framesaws, and the steel spade and iron shovel and three hoes and an axe and tomahawk for each man, and the woollen drawers and worsted stockings for the men, and linsey-woolsey petticoats and caps for the women, and Lieutenant George Worgan's piano,[5] and the rights and obligations that, in being argued back and forth between authority and its many subjects, would make the new place they were coming to so different from the one they left—was this spirit of make-believe, of theatre, of play. And along with it, an audience's delight, and practiced skill no doubt, in watching and listening.

The fact is that the whole of a culture is present, in all its complexity, in small things as well as large. What arrived here with those eleven ships was the European and specifically *English* culture of the late Enlightenment in all its richness and contradiction, however simple the original settlement may have seemed. From the moment of first landing a dense, little new world began to grow up here. Out of the interaction of Europeans with a new form of nature that put to the test all their traditional assumptions about farming methods and how to deal with weather and soil. Out of the interaction of authority with the mass of convicts, around questions of right and obligation, force and consent—these were open questions in some ways because the status of convicts was different here from that of convicts At Home. Out of the interaction between men and women in a place where women were freer than men (they did not have to perform government labour for their food), and freer than women were at home—a good many of these women became independent traders and land holders. Out of the interaction between all these newcomers and those, the original possessors, who were already on the ground. Before long, and well within the first two decades, all the amenities of an advanced society had been conjured up.

Craftsmen of every sort—furniture- and cabinet-makers and long-case clock-makers—had got to work, using Home designs but local woods. Only some of them are known to us by name. John Oatley is one. He made the turret clock that can still be seen in the tympanum of Francis Greenway's Hyde Park Barracks. Then there were brass-founders and tinsmiths, pottery-makers like Samuel Skinner, whose wife Mary took over the business when he died; and quality silversmiths, many of them Irish and most of them transported for forgery, a common crime in that profession. John Austin and Ferdinand Meurant, for example, were both transported from Dublin in 1802 and pardoned two years later, Meurant for knocking £500 off the price of a necklace he made for Governor King's wife. Austin, in a nice colonial irony, went on to become an engraver for the newly established Bank of New South Wales. All these many artisans and makers of fine goods were convicts. They got conditional pardons quickly because the colony needed their skills.

There is something very moving, something we can feel close to, in all this. It speaks of inventiveness and industry beyond the level of mere making do; of a determination to create a world here that would be the old world in all its diversity, but in a new form—new because in these new conditions the old world would not fit. But what is newest of all is the opportunity that was offered to those who might have believed that, in being transported, all future opportunity had been closed to them. In the more relaxed conditions of this new world even convicts had a kind of power they could never have exercised at home. The System had holes—air holes through which a man could catch a second breath and through which a new form of society could be breathed into existence, a society that was rough perhaps, but full as well of the raw energy that comes with opportunity. If I settle on this occasion on just one of this little new world's many re-creations, it is because it seems to me to look forward more evocatively than most to the future, and in a particular way.

In January 1796, just eight years from the beginning, a playhouse was established, a local habitation for that spirit of theatre smuggled in on the *Scarborough*. It was a real theatre, Georgian in design, with a pit, a gallery and boxes. Entrance to the boxes cost five shillings, to the pit two and six, to the gallery a shilling, and those who had no ready cash could pay in kind, that is, in meat, flour or spirits. It was a convict enterprise of the colony's baker, Robert Sidaway, and seems to have established itself (this too might tell us something about the kind of society we were to become) rather more easily than the first church. The Reverend Johnson had to build that for himself, and his first Christmas service, in 1793, drew only thirty-five worshippers. Sidaway's theatre, presumably, did better than that.

An audience is a mysterious phenomenon and subject to mysterious and unpredictable forces. Made up of individuals who shift their attention and their sympathies from moment to moment under the influence of strong emotion or an appeal to their imagination or their sense of humour, but also of a sharpened critical sense in the matter of watching and listening, it is a little society of its own, reconstituted at each performance inside the larger one, and mostly outside its control. Not a mob, but a cohesive unity, with its own interests and loyalties, but unpredictable and therefore dangerous. And this must have been especially true of this audience, composed as it was of convicts and their guards but in convict hands. Fascinating to wonder how far such an audience might constitute the beginnings here of an integrated community, one in which, given the differences—of status, as between convicts and guards, bound and free; of origin, English and Irish; of education, religion, fortune— a various crowd could nonetheless become one.

On 8 April 1800, Shakespeare's *Henry IV Part One* was played. It must have had a special appeal, a special relevance for this audience; one wonders how the authorities allowed it. Political rebellion presented as a falling out between thieves; a tavern underworld of sublime exuberance, where a light-hearted attitude is taken to highway robbery and the picking of pockets; a Lord Chief Justice openly insulted; every sort of high principle roundly mocked. Old hands might have recognised, in the improvised play in which Falstaff and Prince Hal alternately plead for mercy to the King, a version of the mock trials that were one of their chief entertainments in Newgate, a learning-place for first offenders in how to defend themselves in front of the beak. (And Shakespeare's scene may have just such occasions as its reference.) The play's language must have been a particular delight, with its thieves' cant so like the convicts' own 'kiddy' language.[6] And how comically liberating to see lordly authority taken out of the realm of the distantly sacred and brought up close, as they must have seen it every day in the streets of Sydney, in the form of Lieutenant-Governor King, for example, blustering, wrangling, breaking out in the same bad language as themselves.

An extraordinary achievement, and so early in the piece, this alternative stage for action, this exercise in audience-making, society-shaping in the spirit of play. But risky. Dangerous.

Governor King must have thought so anyway. In one of those about-turns that are so common a feature of our history, when all that seems given is taken back again, in September 1800, when his Governorship was confirmed, he closed the playhouse and had it razed to the ground.

A Complex Fate

Writing more than a century ago, when Americans had not yet settled the question of their 'identity' or discovered for themselves an independent role in the world, and when Made in America had not yet become a mark of imperial authority, Henry James spoke of the 'complex fate'[1] of those who are children both of the old world and the new, and of the 'responsibility it entails for fighting against the superstitious valuation of Europe'. What James was concerned with was how, in the face of all that Europe represents in terms of achievement and influence, we are to find a proper value, neither brashly above nor cringingly below its real one, for what belongs to the new world; for what is local but also recent, since part of what is 'superstitious' in our valuation of Europe has to do with the reverential awe we may feel in the presence of mere age. We speak of these places we belong to as new worlds, but what they really are is the old world translated: but *translated*, with all that implies of re-interpretation and change, not simply *transported.* Our ways of thinking and feeling and doing were developed and tested over many centuries before we brought them to this new place, and gave them a different turn of meaning, different associations, a different shape and weight and colour, on new ground.

But the relationship to 'Europe' is only one part of our complex relationship, here, with an anterior world and the intimidating weight of the past. There is also, for us, the example, like a shadow history to be reflected or avoided, of the United States itself.

Australia and the United States are variations, though very different in tone and constitution, on the same original. This means that we share qualities that will always lead us to make comparisons with our American predecessor, forms of social and political thinking that are peculiar enough to keep us close, however we may deviate in practice, and rare enough to be worth noting.

Australia and the United States derive their legal systems from the English Common Law. That is, a system based on precedent rather than principle as in Continental Europe. Each case, as it comes up, is referred back to a previous one, and a judgement arrived at by comparing the two. This preference for the particular over the general has affected more than just the workings of the law. It has kept thinking in both our societies close to example and fact, made it pragmatic and wary of abstractions, and if this has remained stronger in our intellectual life than in the American, it is because we missed the influence of Continental Europe that came early to the United States with successive waves of migration, and especially the one that came with the exodus of so many European intellectuals to America between the two wars. It was an influence we did not feel until the middle 1950s.

Equally important to our two worlds has been the separation of powers we inherited with the British system; and, most important of all, the fact that since the dissolution of Cromwell's New Model Army in the 1650s, no power has ever been accorded to the military. When Australians occasionally play the game of alternative beginnings, of imagining an Australia that might have been French, for example, or Spanish, it is worth reminding them of something. That in failing to be French, we missed out on four bloody revolutions and a couple of by no means benign dictatorships, as well as French food and Gallic stylishness and wit; and in failing to be Spanish spared ourselves an almost continuous history of coups by army factions and rule by military juntas. Stability may be dull, and our society may lack passion—fire in the belly as Manning Clark used to call it—but it does allow people breathing space—and if what this results in is a history without 'interest', it also produces fewer graves. There are not many nations in the world where authority has passed without bloodshed from one administration to the next for more than 150 years, as is true in our case, and more than 200 in the case of the United States. We owe this to the dullness of our British origins.

This shared heritage has made the example of the States an unusually close one. We always have it in mind. When it came to Federation, the American model was clearly one of the possibilities we might have followed and for our Upper House we did take some elements from it. In recent arguments about the republic, the American model of a popularly elected president has seemed to many Australians the one we should in our own way reproduce.

This use of American experience as a reference point for our own goes back to the very beginning.

It was, for example, the British experience of convict transportation to Virginia that determined the new and very different way convicts were dealt with in

New South Wales, and the British Government took great care at the beginning, but also later, not to reproduce in its relations with their new Australian colonies the mistakes that had led to the loss of the American ones. This meant the establishment of freer conditions here, both for convicts and colonists, and this has made a difference.

So did the decision, again a lesson learned from the United States, to use convict labour to establish the colony rather than the labour of slaves. We were saved something in that. A convict, once he has served his time, is free; his children are *born* free. If the convict stain has remained hard to forget and the brutalities, for some, even harder to forgive, it has not been carried down from generation to generation like the stain of slavery.

But if the American model was there as one to be avoided, it also, in other ways, provoked expectations, a good many of which have proved delusory.

The long search in the last century for an inland river system that would water the interior and provide a cheap means for the transportation of goods was based on the analogy of America. So was the idea of an Australia Unlimited, the confident expectation that by the end of the twentieth century Australia would rival and maybe even surpass the United States both in population and power. The hope died hard. When Professor Griffith Taylor, in 1911, made the abominable suggestion that by the year 2000 Australia might have a population of no more than 20 million, he was greeted by howls of patriotic rage and driven out of the country.

Almost from the start, our relationship with America and Americans was a special one, a kind of fraternal twinship. The earliest contact was through the shared industries of whaling and sealing. Later, during the two decades of the gold rushes, there was the movement back and forth between here and California of an army of hungry gold-seekers. This meant not only an extraordinary exchange and mixing of populations, but the introduction into what had been a predominantly English and Irish place of American ways of speech and folk-songs and mythologies: a good many of our folk and work songs come to us in their American version rather than in the original Irish or Scots. All this is part of a continuous cultural relationship, especially with the West Coast, that, out of loyalty perhaps to our British origins, we have allowed in our accounting of these things to be forgotten or suppressed.

San Francisco and Sydney in the nineteenth century were already twin cities. The Lyster Opera Company, for example, which for more than two decades after 1861 provided Sydney and Melbourne with regular opera seasons, had its home base in San Francisco. Australian vaudeville, which was still very much alive here until the late 1950s, was closer in style to American vaudeville than to English Music Hall; and American Country and Western music, after nearly a century of acclimatisation, has become in both senses of the term one of our liveliest indigenous arts. As early as 1827, Peter Cunningham, the convict-ships' surgeon whose *Two Years in New South Wales* is one of the best accounts of life in the colony, writes of the many foreigners who had taken up residence in Sydney. He speaks of French and Germans and Italians, and goes on, 'I had almost said Americans, but kindred ties prevent my ever proclaiming *them* as such'. The kindred tie persisted. When, not long after Federation, the new Australian Government invited the American Fleet to visit, the British had to be assured that this was not—even psychologically, as it clearly was—an attempt on our part to form our own Pacific ties.

There is a sense in which the Australian East Coast and the West Coast of America can be seen as opposite banks of a shared body of water. The reflection back and forth is a strong one, as it has always been, especially if we look these days at the demographic make-up of the two places (the strong presence of Asians, for example, in both populations), or at the lifestyle—surf culture, gay culture, food. (What we call 'modern Australian' cuisine is very like what the Americans call Californian).

Once again the idea of ocean has been essential to

how we define where we are and who it is we are most closely related to. In that shrinking of distance that is a characteristic of our world, even the Pacific, largest of oceans, has become a lake.

All this complicates any argument we might need to make about the 'superstitious valuation' of Europe, or of our colonial link to Britain.

Our fate has been more complex than the American one, as Henry James defined it, and was so from the start. The tension for us is not simply between the old world and the new, or even, as I have been suggesting, between new and newer. Unlike the Americans, we found ourselves in an opposite hemisphere to Europe with opposite seasons, different plants and animals and birds, and different and disorientating stars overhead. This has meant a greater tension, for us, between environment or place on the one hand, and on the other all the complex associations of an inherited culture. We have our sensory life in one world, whose light and weather and topography shapes all that belongs to our physical being, while our culture, the larger part of what comes to us through language for example, and knowledge, and training, derives from another. This is indeed complex, though complexity is not an intolerable burden to minds as flexible as ours— or oughtn't to be. We are amazing creatures, we humans. Our minds can do all sorts of tricks. And this form of complexity, the paradoxical condition of having our lives simultaneously in two places, two hemispheres may be just the thing that is most original and most interesting in us. I mean, our uniqueness might lie just here, in the *tension* between environment and culture rather than in what we can salvage by insisting either on the one or the other.

■　■　■

One of the 'superstitious valuations' I wanted to point to in Henry James's definition of 'complex fate' was that of age as opposed to newness; a valuation, as we have experienced it here, that has sometimes made our 210 years seem too small a purchase on time to constitute a genuine history.

But 210 years is not short. Not if we think of it in terms of lives lived and of all the events and activities and passionate involvements that went into those lives: the things bought and sold, the ideas developed and given a new form, the work, the talk, all that is part of a single life in any single day and which, if we were to grasp the whole of it, we would have to multiply a million times over. Sometimes the only way we can get a sense of those lives and all who lived them, is through the objects, often quite simple objects, that they made and handled. A set of tools, a few shards of pottery, a fragment of wall painting: it may be no more than that, as we know from the way such survivals bring alive for us the 40,000 years of Aboriginal presence in this place.

The truth is that history, as we commonly conceive of it, is not what *happened*, but what gets recorded and told. Most of what happens escapes the telling because it is too common, too repetitious to be worth recording. Even in places like this one where records *are* kept, the history that is in objects may need to be excavated and made visible before we can experience the richness it represents.

When I was growing up 50 years ago, what I now think of as the iconography of Australia—the visual record of all that has been done and made here—had not yet been gathered and made visible. Compared with Europe, the local world we had come out of seemed empty and thin. Now, largely through the work of scholars and museum curators and editors, we can see that that world was not empty at all, but crowded with a making and doing as dense and productive as that of any other offshoot of an advanced civilisation. The evidence now is all about us: in town and country houses and grand public buildings; in country pubs and court houses and fire stations and old stone bridges; in barns, shearing sheds, and bark huts; in the working landscape of ports. In all those necessary objects that make up our sort of living: bookcases and chaise longues and silver trophies and cast-iron railings and shoe buckles and biscuit tins. These things speak to us. They also speak *for* us, and for the many lives that lie behind us and lead up to us.

And 200 years is not so short a time in the life of a city, if we set Sydney and Melbourne, for example, beside Washington or Chicago or Leeds—or, to choose European cities that had their growth in the same period, Budapest and Berlin.

This business of making accessible the richness of the world we are in, of bringing density to ordinary, day-to-day living in a place, is the real work of culture. It is a matter, for the most part, of enriching our consciousness—in both senses of that word: increasing our awareness of what exists around us, making it register on our senses in the most vivid way; but also of taking all that *into* our consciousness and of giving it a second life there so that we possess the world we inhabit imaginatively as well as in fact. This has been especially important in the case of the land itself, and I mean by that everything that belongs to the land: its many forms as landscape, but also the birds, animals, trees, shrubs, flowers that are elements of its uniqueness; and most of all, the *spirit* of the land as it exists in all these things, and can be touched and felt there. Painting can do that for us—we have a long history here of landscape painting. So, with its subtle response to light, can photography. But it is in and through the written word, and especially poetry, that the process works best; this is perhaps because reading is itself an interiorising activity, a matter of 'taking things in'; perhaps because language, with its combination of image and rhythm, its appeal to the eye and to the way our bodies move, is continuous with some activity in us that involves, in the most immediate way, both body and mind.

But the process is not always a simple one. Subtle adjustments may have to be made in the way we look at things before we can bring them within the range of our feelings and then, through words, give them a new life as consciousness.

One of the most eloquent of our early writers is the explorer John Oxley. His *Journals of Two Expeditions into the Interior of New South Wales, 1817-18* is the work of a man of real literary sensibility and an exuberant, if sometimes thwarted, tendency to the romantic.

So long as what lies before him is desolate plains, 'deserts' he calls them, we see him struggling to find words for their undifferentiated dullness and for his own disappointment in them both as explorer and writer. Country of this sort does not need the language he has brought along to describe it. It is unworthy of his generous range of 'feeling'. Each night, like a dutiful schoolboy, he writes up in his journal the landscapes he has crossed. It is heavy going. Then his party gets into rugged mountain country. They see a river that 'entered the glen,' he writes, 'in a fall of vast height … A kangaroo was chased to the fall, down which it leapt and was dashed to pieces—like the hero,' he adds, 'of Wordsworth's "Hart-Leap Well".' This is on 14 September 1818.

Next day, Oxley's whole literary apparatus swings into action at last, and it is the appearance in the landscape of that literary ghost, the enabling image of Wordsworth's hart, as much as the landscape itself, that brings the land he has encountered into the realm of what he can now express.

'Quitting this place,' he writes, 'we proceeded up the glen, into which many small streams fell from the most awful heights, forming so many beautiful cascades. After travelling five or six miles we arrived at that part of the river at which, after passing through a beautiful and level though elevated country, it is first received into the glen. We had seen fine and magnificent falls, each one of which excelled our admiration in no small degree, but the present one so surpassed anything we had previously conceived possible, that we were lost in admiration at the sight of this wonderful natural sublimity.' And there it is at last, the Australian sublime. No sense here of that ironic limiting of Australian possibility (which is also, oddly enough, associated with a kangaroo) in which the earliest of our poets, Barron Field, discovers that the only rhyme our language provides for the continent is 'failure'.

What Oxley reveals is as good an example as we might find, and one that is especially useful because it is so early, of the way a landscape that at first seems unfamiliar and estranging, to lie outside any possibility of response, can be brought into the world of feeling so that it belongs at last to the man who has entered it, so that it comes to exist for him, through the power of words, as a thing *felt*, and therefore fully seen at last, fully experienced and possessed.

Writing in the early 1960s, Judith Wright, who is our best reader of poetry as well as one of our finest poets, pointed out that 'except for the wattle ... there is very little mention of trees, flowers and birds by name or by recognisable description in Australian verse during the nineteenth and early twentieth century'.[2] This is not because they were not there in the landscape, to be seen and appreciated, but because there was as yet no place for them in the world of verse. The associations had not yet been found that would allow them entry there. They carried no charge of emotion. They had as yet played no part in the unfolding human drama. As we saw in the case of Oxley we may need to bring something to natural phenomena before they can reveal themselves to us. As Coleridge puts it, speaking of Nature itself: 'Lady, we receive but what we give'.

In writing of Christopher Brennan and the flowers he uses in his poetry, Judith Wright notes that they have a purely literary provenance; these roses and lilies are the flowers of Swinburne and Tennyson, 'not the familiar and unsung flowers of his new country—flowers which had as yet no ritual or symbolic significance and no meaningful associations in literature, even in the minds of his Australian countrymen'.[3]

In fact, by the time Judith Wright was writing this in 1963 it was no longer true. But only because the poets of her generation—she herself, pre-eminently, but also Douglas Stewart, David Campbell and Roland Robinson, and, when it comes to sea creatures, John Blight—had created a body of poetry in which all the common phenomena of our Australian world—flowers and trees and birds, and helmet shells and ghost-crabs and bluebottles—had been translated out of their first nature into the secondary and symbolic one of consciousness in that great process of culture, and also of acculturation, that creates a continuity at last between the life without and the life within. It is one of the ways—a necessary one—by which we come at last into full possession of a place. Not legally, and not just physically, but as Aboriginal people, for example, have always possessed the world we live in here: in the imagination. And I should just add that I am not suggesting this as yet another and deeper move in the long process of appropriating the continent and displacing its original owners, but as a move towards what is, in effect, a convergence of indigenous and non-indigenous understanding, a collective spiritual consciousness that will be the true form of reconciliation here.[4] That convergence will take place in the imagination, and imagination is essential to it, as Judith Wright saw more than 30 years ago. And poetry is one of the first places where we see it in the making.

Earlier Australian poetry, even the best of Henry Kendall, had scarcely attempted this. The *Bulletin* writers of the 1890s, to quote Judith Wright again, had turned poetry here away from the possibilities of 'philosophy and interpretiveness towards simplicity, vigour and colloquialism', or towards 'sociable yarning', as another critic puts it, 'with a group of mates'. This was a poetry of the outward life, of the soul in *action*, of Paterson's *Clancy of the Overflow* and *The Man from Snowy River.* It took another 40 years, and a poet of great originality—and considering what had gone before, of extraordinary daring—to write a poem that broke out of these manly restrictions and dived inward, claiming for poetry the right to be inward, to be difficult, even obsure, so that the poem might speak for itself at last and get into words what had not yet come into consciousness, what was still 'feeling its way to air'. The poet was Kenneth Slessor; the poem 'South Country'.

> After the whey-faced anonymity
> Of river-gums and scribbly-gums and bush,

After the rubbing and the hit of brush,
You come to the South Country

As if the argument of trees were done,
The doubts and quarrelling, the plots and pains,
All ended by these clear and gliding planes
Like an abrupt solution.

And over the flat earth of empty farms
The monstrous continent of air floats back
Coloured with rotting sunlight and the black
Bruised flesh of thunderstorms:

Air arched, enormous, pounding the bony ridge,
Ditches and hutches, with a drench of light,
So huge, from such infinities of height,
You walk on the sky's beach,

While even the dwindled hills are small and bare,
As if, rebellious, buried, pitiful,
Something below pushed up a knob of skull,
Feeling its way to air.

Landscape in this poem finally gets inside. It would be difficult to say whether what is being presented here is the image of a real landscape—precisely described, objectively there—or an interior landscape just breaking surface, just coming into existence, into apprehension, of which the external one is a reflection. The poem in fact makes no distinction between the two, and part of its beauty and the pleasure it gives us is that it allows us to enter this state, too, in which all tension between inner and outer, environment and being, is miraculously resolved.

'South Country' is an important moment in the development of consciousness in Australia. It is a poem that grants permission to us all to be men and women for whom the inner life is real and matters. And it has a special significance for writers: there is a sense in which the whole of modern Australian writing is 'feeling its way to air' in this poem—and not just poetry either, but fiction as well—in the same way that a whole line of Russian writers, as Turgenev tells us, came out from under Gogol's overcoat. But on this occasion what I want to point to is the resolution of that tension I mentioned between inner life—mind—and the world of objects; between consciousness and environment.

It is in moments of high imagination and daring experiment like the writing of 'South Country' that what Henry James called our 'complex fate' is most clearly visible, but as a tension that has been embraced, as a complexity that has been put to use, a condition made available to all of us as an agency for grounding ourselves both in a particular world and in our own skin.

Landscapes

Towards the end of the sixteenth century, the rich, hardworking little republic of the Netherlands, which was already on its way to becoming the largest economy in Europe, was struck by a craze, which became a mania and led to a second or black economy that threatened to overwhelm the first. It was a craze for tulip bulbs, the rarest of which, by the 1620s, were being exchanged at the rate of a single bulb for a good-sized country estate. At its peak, as on a real stock exchange, only the name of a bulb was needed for a transaction, and an Admiral Bol or an Augustus could change hands for fantastic sums a dozen times in a single day.[1]

This extraordinary phenomenon came about because the tulip, which now grows in vast fields around Lisse and has become, in the popular mind, along with windmills and clogs, a symbol of all things Dutch, was at that time an exotic, brought in, like so many of the plants we associate with the European garden, from the East, in this case from Turkey, via Vienna and Venice, and before that from Persia. Most fruits also came from the East—cherries, peaches, plums, mulberries, apricots—along with a good many of the trees that now make up the recognisable landscapes of the various regions of Europe: the poplars of Lombardy and central and northern France; the umbrella pines of the Mediterranean coast; the cypresses and olives of Provence and Tuscany; the plane trees that shade the streets of London and so many other cities. Imports all, that over the centuries have made the journey west and been acclimatised to create landscapes so deeply associated with particular scenes as to appear essentially and eternally European.

The European landscape is a *made* landscape, a work of 'culture' in both senses of the word.

We need to remember that in the five or six millennia before there were schools of agriculture or bio-technicians, or institutions like the CSIRO, the sophistication of plants and fruits and grasses through which modern foods came into existence was the business of ordinary farmers working with an altogether different form of science: the knowledge that comes from tradition and the questioning of tradition, by trial and error, on the ground.

This is art as well as work. We are makers, among much else, of landscapes. The land under our hands is shaped by the food we eat; by farming methods and ways of preparing and rotating fields; by the ways we hedge or wall or fence them; and by the laws we make for passing them on. We remake the land in our own image so that it comes in time to reflect both the industry and the imagination of its makers, and gives us back, in working land, but also in the idealised version of landscape that is a park or garden, an image both of our human nature and our power. Such making is also a rich form of possession.

Fertility is the essence of it; greenness, both as an actuality and as a metaphor for growth and fruitfulness; a feeling for green seems to be universal in us. And why shouldn't it be? The new leaf, the return of greenness, is a seasonal fact of the world we live in, part of a cycle that gives shape to our lives and to the way we see living itself. Even for desert people an eye of green is the promise of continuity and rebirth. Anyone who has seen an oasis in the desert will know what a miracle it seems, how immediately it lifts the spirits: a garden, which, to make maximum use of the space, is arranged vertically—pomegranates and peaches under stately date-palms, and, in their shade, all mixed in together, every kind of herb and salad vegetable, and geraniums and stocks and daisies. The idea of God's unpredictable bounty, of Grace as some religions conceive it, is only an extension into the spiritual realm of a vivid fact.

And nature in Australia?

Over and over again, what the early settlers and explorers have to say of the landscape they encountered here—Cook and Banks in 1770, Tench in 1788, Oxley on the Western Plains in 1817, Mitchell in Victoria in 1836—was that it resembled, with its half a dozen trees to the acre and its rich grasses, a 'gentlemen's park'. This was the highest form of praise.

What they were referring to was the eighteenth-century style of English landscape gardening as practised by Capability Brown, as opposed for example to the regimented paths and geometric garden beds of Le Nôtre and the Italian gardens of the time, all playful fountains and mythological fantasy. The English garden was an open woodland, planted or improved to look like nature itself, or rather, nature as it appears, in idealised form, in the paintings of Poussin and Claude. What our gentlemen explorers found remarkable was that what in England Nature merely aspired to was in this new place Nature itself.

They were mistaken of course. What they did not see was that this nature, too, was a made one. They did not see it because they did not recognise either the hand of the maker or the method of making. Which was not, as in Europe, by felling with axes what was already there, but by forestalling new growth with the use of fire; by using fire-sticks to create open forests where new grass would attract grazing animals and make spaces wide enough for easy hunting. As Eric Rolls puts it in *A Million Wild Acres*, 'Australia's dense forests are not the remnants of two hundred years of energetic clearing; they are the product of one hundred years of energetic growth' because indigenous people were no longer there to manage them.

The landscape the first settlers came upon was, as we now recognise, a work of land management that native Australians had been practising for perhaps thousands of years. They had over that time created their own version of a useful landscape, a product of culture, and a reflection of it, every bit as much as the Italian or French or English, and may earlier, we now believe, have changed the very form of the continent's vegetation; not by importing new and more competitive species as Europeans did, but accidentally, and once again through their use of fire.

Before their coming, a large part of Australia had been covered with dry rainforest: the *Araucarias* (bunya and hoop-pine) that still cover large areas of southern Queensland and northern New South Wales, and the Antarctic beeches of which a small stand still remains at Springbrook in the hinterland of the Gold Coast. The eucalypt, though it was already on the move, was a minor component of the ancient landscape. The use of fire destroyed the rainforests and favoured the species that were resistent. The eucalypts and sclerophylls took over.

If you drive north from Sydney to Brisbane you come to a natural border, some way south of the political one, where the first bunyas and hoop-pines and silky oaks begin to appear. For me this is always a kind of homecoming to the spirit country of my earliest world, the familiar green, subtropical Australia that was for a long time the only Australia I knew. A world that was always lush green, evergreen.

In a continent as large as ours, there are many kinds of landscape, each of them typical of a particular region, no one more authentically Australian than another. I mention this because I am always taken aback when I hear Australians of a certain turn of mind claim that we will only be fully at home here when we have learned to love our desert places. My Australia, the one I grew up with, and whose light and weather and range of colour shaped my earliest apprehensions of the world, was not dry or grey-green: it was dense and luminous. The old idea that everywhere in Australia looks the same—the myth of the great Australian uniformity—was just that, a myth that was meant, I think, to confirm an Australian need—as if in this too the landscape was to be our model—for a corresponding conformity in the body social and politic. You need to believe in the idea of diversity, perhaps, before you develop an eye for it in the world about you.

We can all learn to appreciate kinds of landscape other than the one we grew up with, to see what is unique and a source of beauty in them. But the landscape we most deeply belong to, that connects with our senses, that glows in our consciousness, will always be the one we are born into.

What the indigenous Australians passed on to us, or rather, what we took from them, was not untouched nature, or at least not in the places where we and they settled, but a *made* nature, which we went on to remake in *our* way.

The land had received the imprint of culture long before we came to it. It had been shaped by use and humanised by knowledge that was both practical and sacred. It had been taken deep into the consciousness of its users so that all its features, through naming and storytelling and myth-making, had a second life in the imagination and in the mouths of women and men.

Here are two visions from that world. The first is an extract from one section of the best known of all Aboriginal song cycles, the Moon Bone Cycle, known, among so many that are not, because it has been so vividly translated for us by the anthropologist, R. M. Berndt:

Up and up soars the Evening Star, hanging there in the sky.
Men watch it, at the place of the Dugong and of the clouds and of the Evening Star,
A long way off, at the place of the mist, of lilies and of the Dugong.
The lotus, the Evening Star, hangs there on its long stalk, held up by the spirits.
It shines on that place of the Shade, on the Dugong place, and on the Moonlight clay-pan.
The Evening Star is shining, back towards Milingimbi, and over the Walamba people.

The second part of Song 30 from the Djanggawal cycle was also translated by Berndt.

We walk along making the country, with the aid of the mauwulan rangga.
We put the point of the rangga into the ground and sing all the way along, swaying our hips.
Oh, waridj Miralaidj, our heads are lolling in weariness!

Our bodies ache after our long journey from Bralgu!
We are making country, Bildjiwuraroiju, the large sandhill
at the place of the mauwulam.[2]

What we did when we came here was lay new forms
of knowledge and a new culture, a new consciousness,
over so much that already existed, the product of
many thousands of years of living in and with the land.
This supplemented what was already there but did
not replace it, and cannot do so as long as any syllable
of that earlier knowledge exists in the consciousness
of even one woman or man.

A land can bear any number of cultures laid one
above the other or set side by side. It can be inscribed
and written upon many times. One of those forms of
writing is the shaping of a landscape. In any place
where humans have made their home, the landscape
will be a made one. Landscape-making is in our bones.

■   ■   ■

I want to go back now to those eleven ships of the
First Fleet and turn to another part of their precious
cargo: the seeds and cuttings, all carefully labelled and
packed, that were to be the beginning of a new
landscape here; all of it the work of one man, Joseph
Banks, President of the Royal Society, founder of the
great gardens at Kew, Cook's companion on the voyage

of 1770 and the man who first suggested Botany Bay as the site for a colony (he had the advantage of having been there).

If Lord Sydney and Governor Phillip were the fathers of the new society that grew up here, Banks is the father of the new natural world that came with it, not just the gardens that Grose saw as early as 1792, and 'that flourish,' as he says, 'and produce fruit of every variety—vegetables are here in great abundance', but, in time, of the wheatlands of the Darling Downs and the Western Plains; the orchards of Tasmania and the Riverina and the Granite Belt in Queensland; the vineyards of the Hunter and the Barossa and Margaret River in the west. Of the tree plantings, too, in country towns, some now so old and established as to form part of our national heritage; of our Botanical Gardens; and of that special fondness we have here for exotic imports from South America and South Africa and Asia: the jacarandas we like to plant so that they will bloom in vivid combination with our native flame trees, the bauhinias and poincianas and African tulip trees of our suburban streets, the camphor laurels and Benjimani figs and deodars of older gardens.

We can imagine Banks, the '*amoroso* of the Tahitian Islands' as Manning Clark called him, 15 years after he had last been there, stepping back in imagination to the far side of the globe to play a godlike little game with himself and with a whole continent, and doing what no man in history had ever done before: telescoping into a few hours and a single occasion what might have taken centuries—millennia even—in the natural course of things: the equipping of an arkload of plants suitable for a place, as he recalled it, with 'a climate similar to that of southern France'—apples, cherries, apricots, nectarines; red and white beets, early cauliflower, celery, sainfoin; nasturtium, broccoli, York cabbage—the makings of very practical little garden of Eden, with due care taken for the good health of those it was to feed, and with nice problems to be solved on the ground, since only trial and error and a flair for inventiveness and guesswork, would determine which of the several varieties he had chosen would actually 'take' in a place where the soil and seasons were as yet unknown; where the soil, as it turned out, lacked minerals and large animals to manure it, and the seasons were not an alternation of hot and cold, as in Europe, but of wet and dry.

Some of these plants had already made the slow journey westward from China and Persia, and had travelled on from Europe to the new Europe of the Americans. Others—tomatoes and maize and peppers and potatoes—had made the journey in the other direction, from west to east. Now they were to feed the even newer Europe in Australia. They were to make the landscape we all live in here—and live off as well—and whose produce we have sent out for the best part of 150 years to clothe and feed the world.

All this once seemed a bold and triumphant exercise, typical of the belief, which has been central to our culture, that Nature is there for our delight and use, to be adapted and improved and made fruitful; the belief that intervention in the workings of Nature—by divine injunction in the seventeenth century, out of civic duty later—is part of what it is to be human.

These days we are less sure. This is because we have begun to be aware at last of what such radical intervention may mean, especially in a continent like ours that has turned out to be more fragile than we first understood and less naturally suited than we believed to the kinds of farming and pastoralism we have imposed upon it. Eric Rolls, a poet as well as an historian, who writes better about the Australian landscape, with more affection and a keener eye for its intimate life than any other man here, describes what the earliest settlers found when they first came upon it: 'The surface was so loose that you could rake it through the fingers. No wheel had marked it, no leather heel, no cloven foot—every mammal, humans included, had walked on padded feet. Our big animals did not make trails. Hopping kangaroos usually move in scattered company, not in damaging single file like sheep and cattle … Every grass-eating mammal had two sets of teeth to make a clean bite. No other land had been treated so gently.'[3]

The damage since has been severe: the breaking up of the soil and the trampling of the grass by hoofed animals, indiscriminate clearing, erosion, the draining of swamps that has led to salination through a rise in the water table, the damage to our rivers through excessive irrigation and through chemical pollution.

This depredation of the environment is one reason why we no longer feel triumphant. Another is the doubt many of us now have about whether our way of doing things is the *only* way, the only *human* way— a doubt, by the way, that would not have occurred to our predecessors. It only occurs to us because we began, a few decades ago, to interest ourselves in comparative anthropology, in the way other cultures see the world and interact with it.

We live in close proximity here to a people whose way of looking at things is quite different from ours; and while they have not lived entirely without intervening in the workings of Nature, they have, in fact, dealt gently with it, and, in their long experience of the place have learned a thing or two about how to live in co-operation with its strange and unpredictable ways. We now recognise this.

Nature once seemed all-powerful, a force before which man, with his puny strength, was entirely vulnerable. These days, in one of those odd reversals that occur in human thinking, it is Nature itself that seems vulnerable—fragile, precarious, constantly in need of our protection and care. Its resources no longer seem infinite. We need to preserve and protect them if we ourselves are to survive, and to do this we need to listen carefully to what the experts have to tell us, and to both sides when they disagree. To many people who care about these things it is already too late to save the continent and, as some of them insist, the planet itself. Eric Rolls, in his quiet and pragmatic way, is more reassuring. 'It is not too late,' he tells us, 'to make corrections, the knowledge is available'.[4]

It is partly because Rolls is by nature so reasonable, partly because he has himself been a farmer, that he is unwilling to ascribe all that has been done here to contempt for the land or to simple greed; nor does he put Nature's needs at every point before our need to feed ourselves. 'The greatest song of the land', he writes, 'is the food it produces. One cannot blame European settlers for bringing in the livestock and plants that have done so much damage here, it would have been unnatural for them to settle in a new country without the feed that they knew.'[5] Rolls is passionate but he is neither evangelical nor apocalyptic. The important thing for him is that the way we use the land should be sensible and informed. But there are many people for whom nature in these last years has become the last repository of the sacred. Saving it, saving every last scrap of it, every species, every tree and plant, is a religious duty. The struggle between farmers and conservationists, loggers and conservationists, developers and conservationists, has become for them another and later version of the old fight between moral and spiritual purity on one hand and on the other the devil's work that is inherent in the day-to-day business of being in the world. Evangelical and apocalyptic language, and a hectoring self-righteousness, powers their energy and gives shape to their arguments.

The fervour is understandable and may even be necessary; but self-righteousness is not a pretty phenomenon. Neither is religion when it develops an edge of fanaticism. I am thinking of those holy vandals of the late sixteenth and early seventeenth century who, out of pure Protestant zeal, knocked the heads off statues in Lady Chapels and smashed every stained-glass window in East Anglia.[6] Our culture is subject to these waves of purifying zeal, and Australia has not been exempt in the past from outbreaks of radical purity. Wowserism at the end of the last century led a crusade against drink, sex and every form of pleasure, and imposed a censorship here that lasted for more than 60 years. A fanatical racism once seemed inseparable from the very idea of nationhood. It would rigorously have excluded Asians, blacks, Jews, and such 'inferior' southern Europeans as Italians, Greeks and Maltese, in the attempt to preserve a purity of race that would guarantee for Australians an eternally white and, if possible, eternally Protestant history.

In their latest incarnation these puritanical exclusionists have chosen Nature as their sphere. Their aim is the expulsion from our parks and gardens and foreshores of every bush, plant and flower that is not a *bona fide* native. Not so much out of concern for the health of the environment, the need to conserve water, for example—though that is sometimes a part of the argument—as for the health of the nation, our sense of ourselves as Australians. Only when the last non-native shrub and flower has been grubbed out of the earth, and our hearts no longer leap up at the sight of a daffodil or a bed of tulips at the Canberra Floriade, will we have broken free at last of the old superstitious nostalgia for Europe and be ourselves natives, at least in spirit, of our Australian land. This is the most fundamental form of an argument that only what belongs uniquely to this place, that derives all its elements from the *life* of the place, can be authentically Australian. That Australia must be kept free of all alien pollutants and influences. That if we, as individuals and as a nation, are to be unique, only the uniqueness of the land can shape us.

This may present itself as an authentically local passion, but is more culturally determined than its adherents suspect. What is new in it is the strong associations carried by the word 'native'. Once applied only to Aborigines, it was appropriated by the first generation of the native-born as a sign of their difference from settlers and other imports, and as a claim to belonging. We have long since given up that claim to it; we no longer speak of ourselves as 'native'. Perhaps, as some of our radical conservationists use the term, we are meant to see in the exclusive claim of 'natives' to a place here, not only an argument about the land but a restorative gesture towards its original owners. The gesture may be a noble one, but is not, in its exclusiveness, in the spirit of Aboriginal thinking about these matters. That seems more concerned, in its pragmatic way, with what is now here and on the ground, with re-imagining the scene to include all that is now in it, than with looking back nostalgically to what was there 20 or even 200 years ago. This capacity to re-imagine things, to take in and adapt, might be something we should learn from, something that comes closer than a nostalgia for lost purity to the way the world acutally is, and also to the way it works. It might remind us as well of something we need to keep in mind: which is the extent to which Aboriginal notions of inclusiveness, of re-imagining the world to take in all that is now in it, has worked to include *us.*

Writing of an early moment in our history, Alan Atkinson, in *The Europeans in Australia*, speaks movingly of Bennelong's relations with Phillip, and suggests that Bennelong may have made a larger leap in incorporating Phillip into his world, in opening his view of things to include all that Phillip stood for, than the Governor or any of his officers had to make to find a place for him.

They had come here *expecting* to find natives. They had an impeccable document that outlined how they should deal with them, and knew, either from previous experience or from their reading in Montaigne and Shakespeare and Rousseau, and from Defoe's *Robinson Crusoe*, what a native might be, and from Cook and Banks what *these* natives might be. But Bennelong was not expecting this meeting. He had no preparation for it but his own capacity to observe, open his imagination, and respond.

What he made of Phillip, the room he made in his world for Phillip's authority and for Phillip's house as a 'sacred site' (he was eager, for example, that his daughter should be born in its grounds), speaks for an act of accommodation, of inclusiveness, that is an example to each one of us, and, considering all that followed, a shame to each one of us as well. But Bennelong, however weak he may have been in physical power, had behind him the strength of a culture that in being old had developed, in its long view of things, an extraordinary capacity to accept change and take in what was new and must be adapted to. It is in terms of that long view that what we have made here will be judged; and in the shaping of a collective consciousness, mixed but truly native, Bennelong's inclusive view, his imaginative leap, may turn out to have been the most important element in that first and fateful meeting of two worlds.

Monuments to Time

The Brisbane I grew up in in the late 1930s and early 1940s was a sprawling, subtropical town with a style of domestic architecture that was all its own, and which comes as close as we get here to an urban vernacular. One-storeyed weatherboard, with a tin roof, verandahs, and, since the house sits high on stumps, an under-the-house closed in with lattice, it is a style that is directly responsive to the climate and to the city's hilly terrain, and makes use as well of local timbers: hardwood for the weatherboard exterior, hoop-pine for the interior tongue-and-groove. The same materials were also used on a larger scale for churches, including some high-pitched, turreted affairs that are their own form of antipodean Gothic.

If anything made me aware of being an Australian, and specifically a Queenslander, it was the house I grew up in. I have written elsewhere of how its spaces determined early habits of living, of mapping the world, as well as my first sensory responses, of the way that living, as we did, in weatherboard houses on high stumps creates a certain sort of consciousness.

> They have about them the improvised air of tree-houses. Airy, open, often with no doors between the rooms, they are on such easy terms with breezes, with the thick foliage they break into at window level, with the lives of possums and flying-foxes, that living in them, barefoot for the most part, is like living in a reorganised forest. The creak of timber as the day's heat seeps away, the gradual adjustment in all its parts, like a giant instrument being tuned, of the house-frame on its stumps, is a condition of life that goes deep into consciousness. It makes the timber-house dweller, among the domes- ticated, a distinct subspecies.[1]

But the truth is that most people in my youth were ashamed of this local architecture. Timber was a sign of poverty, of our poor-white condition and back-wardness: it made 'bushies' of us. Safe houses, as everyone knows, are made of brick—think of the *Three Little Pigs*. Timber is primitive. The fact that you could, on any day of the week in Brisbane, see a whole house being carted through the streets on the back of a lorry suggested there was something impermanent, makeshift, about these dwellings, but also about the places where they were set down. Queensland was full of ghost towns whose houses had been carted off to make a new town elsewhere. It wasn't until the late 1960s that our shabby weatherboards got a new lick of paint, a new name— Old Queenslanders—and Brisbane's beautiful inner suburbs, with tin roofs flashing in the gullies among paw paw, mango and banana trees, or on hilltops among the original hoop-pines and bunyas, were recognised at last as interesting, even unique, and our comfortable weatherboards as one of the dis-tinctive forms of domestic architecture, variously produced from state to state, that represent one of our most original achievements as Australians and a happy addition to the local scene.

Even when the basic style is imported, as in the case of the Sydney terrace, local taste and the up-and-down streets give it a different rhythm from the British original, and the decoration a new and less formal accent.

A Sydney terrace is not at all like a terrace in Liverpool or Newcastle upon Tyne. Not least in the profusion, the sense of fantasy, of the lions and urns and flames that are used for its finials, and the flamboyance with which its cast-iron balconies celebrate local flora in the form of ferns and lilies, or ethnic identity in thistles and Irish harps. If we need a reference for such originality in the adaptation of an imported style, we might find it in the colonial houses of the United States, whose lovely incongruity lies in their being built in a correct Queen Anne or Georgian style, but in timber rather than brick, then painted bright yellow or emerald green or burgundy. It makes them, if we know the original, look problematical and wrong—a mistake, it might seem, or a provincial joke. But because of their lightness, the confidence with which they are set down in the new place and the rightness of their colours in the watery light, the old style translated becomes something fresh and original.

I took our weatherboard house for granted. I didn't think it particularly beautiful—I barely thought of it at all. It was simply where we lived, the only house I had ever known. What I did think about, and puzzle over, when I looked at Brisbane and asked myself what sort of city I was growing up in, was our public buildings.

Built for the most part between separation, in 1859, and the late 1880s when Brisbane was not much more than 20,000 souls, they *were* of stone, local sandstone; big, imposing monuments to—to what?

In a variety of styles—Italian Renaissance, French Renaissance, Palladian—that had little to do with the real history of a place that had only recently been reclaimed from densely wooded, subtropical rain-forest, they were, it seemed to me, incongruously and pretentiously plonked down where they simply did not belong.

They were impressive, certainly, you could not miss that; or their confidence. Solid gestures towards the future, they were the landmarks of a city that had not yet come into existence, the 'grand centre of civilisation', to steal Darwin's phrase, that would one day grow up around them and, leaving behind at last the memory of tin-roofed stores and weatherboards and verandahed pubs, be equal at last to what their builders had in mind. They belonged to Time rather than Space. To a city that even in my youth had not yet seized the occasion to appear.

If our flimsy wooden houses were the product of geography, of a response to climate and to the peculiar topography of the place, these grand public buildings were the product of history, of that form of it called culture. But to what extent could one think of them as local and Australian rather than as impressive repro-ductions of a more real and authentic Over There?

That others of my generation shared these doubts is revealed by the number of these grand old buildings that were pulled down in the 1950s and 1960s to make way for architecture that was more modern, more 'appropriate'.

The results for Sydney were devastating. Half the nineteenth-century city was destroyed. It might just as well have had its heart ripped out under the fury of aerial bombardment. The line of buildings that still remain along Macquarie Street and around Bent and Bridge Streets, and the single block of the Queen Victoria Building, show us something of what was lost.

Other places fared better. In Adelaide most of King William Street has survived, and so has North Terrace. And until the oil and mineral boom of the late 1960s, Brisbane too escaped. Brisbane and Adelaide were poor. Sydney, in the 1960s, the decade of the Southern Vandals, had the misfortune to be rich.

So what I have to say is in some ways an attempt at reparation, a late tribute to what, 40 years ago, I did not recognise because I did not have the eyes as yet to see what was there.

I had known these buildings for as long as I could remember. A nervous 10-year-old, I had stood in the middle of the big empty ballroom at Old Government House on a cold winter's afternoon and bowed my way through the studies and solo pieces I had chosen for the AMEB music exams. On hundreds of afternoons on my way home from school, I had waited for the West End tram outside the old Treasury Building.

Among so much that was merely patched together and rotting and peeling, they had such an air of permanence, these old buildings, the Customs House, the Post Office, Parliament House. They were the nearest thing we had to something ancient and historical. What disturbed me most, I think, was that I had always found them beautiful, even moving, but I distrusted their beauty and could not understand why I was moved. If I do now, it is because I have liberated myself from the narrow assumptions about what is appropriate, or authentic, that then prevented me from seeing what these buildings were doing, what they were for. But to see that I had to look elsewhere.

■　■　■

In the early eighteenth century Lord Burlington and his followers had begun to build country houses in England in the style of the Venetian architect Palladio, a style already 100 years old when they took it up,[2] and itself a kind of folly; a fantasia, though a very restrained one, on classical themes, which Palladio had translated from an imaginary south, all bosky groves and warm honeyed light, and set down among the misty valleys and hills of the Veneto. Burlington translated the style to the Home Counties, where it established itself so thoroughly in the form of winged villas and arcaded loggias that it became the prevailing

British style for the next century and a half, and in this form was exported to Australia. To Queensland, for example, where it was used, in the 1860s, for one of Brisbane's earliest and most beautiful buildings, Old Government House.

That the style did not at first sit easily with the English climate is suggested in Pope's gentle mockery of those who built, as he says:

> Long arcades through which the cold winds roar,
> Proud to catch cold at a Venetian door.[3]

What were the English Palladians doing with this late Renaissance version of the classical? That it *was* classical gives us the clue.

The late seventeenth and early eighteenth centuries in England were a time when the classical world, and particularly Augustan Rome, the age of Virgil and Horace, represented the ideal of elegance and achieved order and beauty, and a model of what the civilised and civilising spirit might achieve, not only in poetry but in all the arts. Palladianism was the equivalent in architecture of the heroic couplet—of Pope's *Moral Essays* and *The Rape of the Lock*, works whose tone might be playful, mock-heroic as well as heroic, but whose intention was always serious. It was an attempt to claim for eighteenth-century England a continuity, not as historical continuity, but one of the spirit, with

Augustan Rome, to recreate Roman ways of thinking and feeling, Roman virtues, on English soil. In this the particulars of climate and place were irrelevant. It was a matter of imagination, of mind, and Palladio had already shown the way. If classical forms could be translated from the heat and glare of the south to misty Venice, then why not to misty Buckinghamshire?

The point of these arcaded villas and domed rotundas was not to *express* place but to redefine and transcend it. By setting a Palladian building down on English soil, what might be coaxed from the English landscape were the qualities of an Italian one; not as they existed in any real place, even in Italy, but as they appeared, along with the usual Virgilian and Arcadian associations, in the idealised landscapes of Poussin and Claude.

It is in the light of this view of architecture, this way of using it to exert a force on the sites it occupied, that I came to look again—but really for the first time—at my Brisbane buildings.

To take the immediate example of Old Government House: far from being an example of servile colonialism or a nostalgic glance towards the Home Counties, its Palladian pretensions quite out of place in subtropical Queensland, mightn't we see it as doing just what the same style had done for Burlington—claiming for this new place a continuity with the classical world and its values (Governor Bowen, who built it, was a renowned classicist), imposing on the local landscape—in this case Brisbane's old Botanical Gardens with their bamboos and Moreton Bay figs and hoop-pines and bunyas—the aesthetic order of Poussin and Claude, and in this way legitimising, domesticating within the arcadian world of those classical painters, Brisbane's exotic flora and tempestuous late-afternoon skies? Governor Bowen, who was fond of drawing a comparison, both topographical and climatic, between Queensland and Naples, might even have seen it as restoring the style to an original, 'Mediterranean' environment where it was more at home than it could be either in southern England or the Veneto.

Of course, this kind of thinking is very far from the theories about building that have prevailed in our own century, in which architectural forms are related in an organic way to the landscape they stand in, or emerge directly from it. Only recently has post-modernism, with its eye for the playfully eclectic, raised the possibility of a different way of looking at things, one that has allowed us to regard our older buildings with renewed interest, as products of an age when architectural design was a matter of spirited play—between landscape and architecture, style and history, history and function; but *strong* play, play with a purpose, play as an act of appropriation.

I am speaking here of a time when Australia saw itself not as a primitive outpost of the known world but as a full participant in all that was happening in an exciting and expansive age. It was remote certainly, but not for that reason either behind the times or out of competition with what was being done on the international scene. If public buildings in our cities presented a set of variations on past historical styles, this was not out of nostalgia for someone else's history or because the place lacked a history of its own, but because it saw itself as being up with the contemporary. Men built here as they were building at the time in Paris and Vienna and Budapest. On the same principle and in pretty much the same styles.

This feeling for period, and for period styles, was something new. A sense of history, of what is alive and accessible in past times and past objects, has not always been part of our sensibility. Until well into the nineteenth century, things were either ancient—that is, classical—or they were modern. Only the antique was capable of eliciting a romantic response, and this was almost entirely literary. Greek and Roman ruins were eloquent, they spoke to the heart, because they belonged to the world of Virgil and Homer. No such associations were evoked by the gothic. The medieval world of heraldry and castles and tournaments and chivalry had not yet become, as it was to be later, the repository of everything noble and picturesque, the great spiritual escape from industry and steam. Gothic buildings, which were invariably in a poor state of repair, were merely decrepit and old. Relics of a dead past and an age that, for modern taste, was primitive and barbaric, they were leftover rubbish taking up space that might better be filled with the living, with what belonged to the new world of light and speed.

When Victor Hugo began *The Hunchback of Notre Dame*, in 1829, the great cathedral that stood at the centre of his book was a dilapidated ruin. Solemn and neglected, in a style that spoke too clearly of ancient unrefinement and a brutality for which modern people of cultivation could feel only a fastidious revulsion, it was an embarrassment, an ignominious wreck. It was Hugo's extraordinary imagination that restored its grandeur and mystery and made Notre Dame, with its fantastic waterspouts and gargoyles, its buttresses and high inner spaces, the embodiment, for a new generation, of the very spirit of Paris. The vast popularity of Hugo's novel made Gothic (with a capital letter now) the high point of all that was finest in the recent past, and French Gothic the highest achievement of French civilisation. This was one of the great revolutions of the age.

But for the men who remade Paris and London in the 1840s and 1850s, the old was simply old: filthy alleys that clogged the city with foul odours, tenements that were the breeding ground of crime and every sort of infectious disease. They had no compunction about clearing away such rubbish so that these great cities could be what every city aspired to be—which is modern.

Balzac had written evocatively of the old Paris, as Dickens did of London, but very little of what they describe survived their lifetimes. The wooden galleries of *Lost Illusions*, the original of Tom-all-Alone's in *Bleak House*, the nightmarish bridges and walkways across which the Artful Dodger leads Oliver in *Oliver Twist*—all were swept away by the new science of town planning to make apartment blocks or residential squares for the expanding middle class, and thoroughfares, boulevards, for traffic, or to clear a path for the railways and a space for those temples to Progress, the big, new terminal stations. As late as 1871, when the Tuileries and the Hôtel de Ville were damaged during the Paris Commune, the authorities thought them not worth preserving, although they were by no means irreparable.

To have none of these old relics to deal with was to a city's advantage. The Australian cities, along with newly laid out, post-industrial cities like Leeds, Manchester and Newcastle upon Tyne, which until recently had been little more than large villages, had the good fortune to be modern already, and Melbourne thought of itself as having the edge on Sydney because it had been planned from the start, whereas the elder city had grown up higgledy-piggledy and had much early rubbish to remove.

Vienna offers a good example of the way the age looked at things.

When the medieval walls of Vienna were pulled

down in the late 1850s to make way for the Ring-strasse, most of what remained of the pre-Baroque city went with them. What was raised in its place was 'modern'. That is: the Opera House was neo-Baroque, the National Theatre and the two great Museums, as befits houses of culture, were neo-Renaissance, the Town Hall and the University neo-Gothic, and the Parliament Alexandrian Greek.

Now the Austro–Hungarian Empire, in point of fact, has no more direct relationship with ancient Greece than Australia has, or the United States; but classical Greek seemed as right, in the Kaiserlich and Königlich nineteenth century, as a gesture towards liberal dem-ocracy, as it had earlier for the Capitol in Washington and the Assemblé Nationale in Paris. In the same way, Gothic, on the model of Oxford and Cambridge and Marburg and Göttingen, seemed right for a university, not only in Vienna but all over the world.

I have gone this long way about to create as precisely as I can the contemporary context—the idea of a city, and specifically a modern city—in which we need to place Australian buildings of the period if we are to see what their makers had in mind, the claim these government offices and banks and stock exchanges and galleries and museums were making for Australia as an internationally up-to-date place, and as Europe translated. The claim was to the continuation of an ideal rather than an actual history; the same claim that was being made in Paris or Vienna, where after all a real history, if that was what you wanted, was already available on the ground.

What we are dealing with here is an Australia that saw itself, in cultural terms, not as colonial but as confidently provincial, standing in the same relationship to London as the great provincial cities of England, or, to put it another way, as Palmyra or Baalbek or Leptis Magna did to second-century Rome. A lack of history can free you from history by leaving you free to play with the historical and construct an ideal history of the spirit or mind.

When I look again at Brisbane's most triumphant building, J. J. Clarke's Treasury[4]—it is now the Brisbane Casino; we too have our playful mode—what I see is an attempt, a bold one, very forward looking and ideas driven, to claim for this site above the river, and for what till then had been a town of unsealed streets and only the most modest timber dwellings, the sort of Italianate possibilities that go with its grandeur of design; the entrepreneurial energies of Italian Renaissance bankers, the independence and enterprise of the Italian city-states. It is a matter of using style, conjoined with function, to exert force on a site, and to open up within it a whole range of social and economic possibilities. It would be quite wrong to see such a building as offering a comfortable evocation of the European and familiar—to see it, I mean, as nostalgic. It is too commanding for that. It exerts too strong a force, establishes too many tensions, speaks too boldly of ambition and local power. Like the gem-like Customs House in the next bend of the river, its aim is to redefine the site by deepening its associations in a way that will make the building's uses seem natural, sanctioned by long association, and in that way to appropriate a future for it. But its aim is also to make the site itself more complex, and open therefore to possibilities, adding to climate and vegetation a cultural dimension, and shifting what can be seen—the site's natural history—in the direction of what is there as yet only in potential, a future that will be determined not by nature or past history but by the calling of new forces on to the scene.

■　■　■

The scene.

If there is something of the theatrical, something of the stage-set about these buildings, then that surely is part of the intention. They are, like a stage-set, meant to be both a proper scene for action and an inspiration and guide to action, encouraging, by their very size and assurance, but most of all by the references inherent in their style, a grandeur and confidence of gesture that might push a man towards illustrious performance. In the same way, Gothic halls of residence,

Gothic cloisters and quadrangles, were meant, by a kind of associative process, to encourage a devotion to scholarly excellence. The set was there, it was up to those who entered it to fill the scene with appropriate action. These buildings have an air of magic as well as theatre about them. They are magic boxes, a good part of their function as galleries, banks, city halls, treasuries, parliaments being to give those who entered them access to power, which they would acquire by setting themselves in the line of a powerful continuity.

What I have been looking back to is a time when culture, as it was embodied in our long European inheritance, was the determining factor in the creation of our Australian world. In the choice between culture on the one hand, and geography on the other, the nineteenth century comes down firmly on the side of culture, on what belongs to mind. Arguing from there made nineteenth-century Australia confident because powerful. Even over-confident. The idea grew up that if we could only keep ourselves pure in a contaminated world—morally pure, but racially pure, too—it would one day be our privilege, as a nation, to carry forward into history the British ideal.

But this ambition for empire, for a manifest destiny, came at a price. It introduced a note of anxiety, which deepened, and has never gone away.

Strange as it may seem at this distance, we were most confident, most sure of where we stood, both as regards space and time, when we saw ourselves in a provincial relationship to a world that was itself central and stable. The desire to stand alone, to have a destiny and a history of our own, was inevitable of course, and necessary, but it destabilised us, introducing first a resentful sense of being marginal, of being colonial and irrelevant to the main course of things, then an endless worrying back and forth about how we were to ground ourselves and discover a basis for identity. Was it to be in what we had brought to the place or what we found when we got here? Was cultural inheritance to define us, even in the radically changed form that being in a new place demanded, or the place itself?

But the belief that we must make a choice is an illusion, and so, I'd suggest, if we are to be whole, is the possibility of choosing. It is our complex fate to be children of two worlds, to have two sources of being, two sides to our head. The desire for something simpler is a temptation to be *less* than we are.

Our answer on every occasion when we are offered the false choice between this and that, should be, 'Thank you, I'll take both'.

The Orphan in
the Pacific

The 1950s, precisely because they mark a watershed in the life of modern Australia, have become a disputed area. They are for some the last time in our history when old-fashioned frugality and a sense of duty mattered to people; when you could still leave the front door open while you slipped down to the shops; when it was still shameful to be divorced; when gentlemen still gave up their seats to ladies on the tram; when backyards in the cities still had a vegetable patch, and a wire-netting enclosure for chooks, that kept city folk in touch with country matters and made city kids aware of where eggs come from and that the chicken they were eating once had a head—though not perhaps what any four-year old today could tell them, which is where they themselves had come from, unless it was from under one of the cabbages their dad grew down the back.

It was the last time, too, when most Australians shared the same culture; that is, when there was no significant divide between high and low culture, and none, certainly, between youth culture and the rest. When families had their own seats at the Saturday-night pictures and were loyal to the Regent or the Metro whatever film was on. When the races dominated the radio on Saturday afternoons and everyone had the number of an SP bookie. When rodeos were still a city spectacle, and English comedy-shows such as *Much Binding in the Marsh* and *Take It from Here*, and vaudeville houses with their strong flavour of vernacular humour had not yet been replaced by American sitcoms, and we still told Dad and Dave or Dave and Mable jokes, most of them dirty.

At sixteen, as I was in 1950, I could mix Tex Morton, big band jazz, and Gladys Moncrieff in *Rio Rita*, with the Top Twenty, the Amateur Hour, the Lux Radio Theatre, the Borovanski Ballet, the surf every weekend, and the last episodes of *The Search for the Golden Boomerang*—all with no sense that I was doing anything but responding to what most interested and amused me. High culture was there— Australia in those years was still on the international circuit; in the late 1940s I heard almost every great conductor and instrumentalist of the day—but it was simply part of the mix. So were we. I had not yet discovered that names I had known all my life like Uscinski and Rasmussen and Reithmuller were 'foreign', or that my own name was as well. It didn't feel foreign and was so common around Brisbane that most people did not take it that way. All very comfortable, it sounds, and secure and cosy. Still, I have other memories of the time that are none of those.

Like most young people, I saw the world as excitingly new and full of possibility, but what struck me in the adult world around me was a kind of anxiety at the centre of people's lives, a sense of resentment, of disappointment or hurt; a prickliness, too, that could easily become mean-spirited mockery and contempt for anything 'different'—large gestures, extravagant emotions; a suspicion of everything 'out there' that might challenge our belief that the world we had here, however ingrown and pinched it might seem to outsiders, was the biggest, the fairest, the sunniest, the healthiest, the best fed.

What was it that had scared us? What were we afraid of?

Communism, of course. Reds, both outside and, more insidiously, within. The infection of Europe: all those recent horrors that we imagined might be brought in, like germs, with those who were fleeing from them. The sick disorder and obscenity of Modernism, and especially of *modern art*, whose cleverness and assault on traditional beliefs and values, we thought, were meant to make fools of us. Well, we were *not* fooled! American culture and commercialism. But there were some of us who were also in love with it: American pop songs and musicals, American writing, American style in the way of Levi jeans and Cornel Wilde haircuts, American films—though much that we took to be American, as it came to us from the Hollywood dream factory, was shot through with the darker tones of Europe. It was in the popular and commercial form of the movies, held in such contempt by local intellectuals, that we had our first contact with forms of modernism—contemporary music, for example, or German Expressionism—from which we were otherwise protected.

It seems to me now to be a world that was forever crouched in an attitude of aggrieved and aggressive self-defense. Closed in on itself. A stagnant backwater and sullenly proud of the fact. A world that had not come to terms with wounds, deep ones, that something in the national psyche, or our digger code, did not allow us to speak about or even to feel as deeply as we might need to do, if we were to be whole again.

The lack of a tradition in our writing for dealing with anything but the external life, manly action in the open, meant that the experience of the trenches, that moment in Western history when a break occurred in our long-held belief in progress and the benign nature of technology, went unexpressed here. There was no local equivalent of the poetry of Wilfred Owen or of *All Quiet on the Western Front.* The horror, the deep pain of that experience, was not recreated here in the kind of imaginative form that allows a society to come to terms with itself by taking what it has suffered deep into its consciousness and reliving it there in the form of meaning rather than as muddle and shock.

We began to think of ourselves as having been betrayed. Of our willingness, our good nature, as having been taken advantage of. At Gallipoli. In the last days of the war in France, when we had made so large a sacrifice but received so little acknowledgment of it. At the Peace Conference afterwards, where the British had thwarted our attempts to acquire the German possessions in the Pacific, and granted those that lay north of the equator to the Japanese, thus bringing one step closer what most Australians saw as a potential aggressor.

Events out there seemed to have developed a quality that reduced us, for all our larrikin assurance and swagger, to victims. There was the death overseas, among strangers as we thought of it, of Phar Lap and Les Darcy. There was the swamping of our cinema industry, which had begun so strongly and was so lively and confident, by the superior power, the money power, of Hollywood. There was the Bodyline series. All these blows, large and small, had shaken our confidence, made us bitter, made us draw back in distrust of the world, but also of ourselves and of one another.

Of course there was also the censorship: on books, on films, on any idea that might corrupt us morally or shake the society up by questioning values so firmly entrenched, so universally accepted, that to go against even the least of them might begin a fragmentation that could never be repaired.

To read *Ulysses* you had to get permission from the State Librarian, who kept it under lock and key in the office. It was not for sale. And it was still forbidden to advertise condoms (men and boys got them 'under the counter' at the barbers) or to publish information of any kind about birth control. In Queensland, where I lived, in an odd reversal of what everywhere else in the world is regarded as civilised behaviour, the law forbade us to eat and drink on the same premises.

It is easy to laugh at these foolish restrictions. But they were only the visible sign of something larger and more insidious—more disabling, too. A sense of embattlement against life itself, a fear not just of the threat from without, but of the even darker forces that lurked within. We were terrified, I think, of discovering that the body, for all our shame and fear of it, was harmless; that pleasure, too, might be harmless; and that ideas, even dangerous ideas, ones that put us at risk, might be as essential to our wholeness and good health as cod-liver oil or Vegemite. Meanwhile, it seemed, only the acceptance of a strict conformity would save us from ourselves and society from a collapse into total degeneracy: National Service, a vote for Mr Menzies, and moral and legal restrictions backed up by a system of official and unofficial pimping and prying that used nice-looking young policemen to entrap homosexuals in public lavatories, and divorce agents, hired by the 'aggrieved party', to burst into hotel bedrooms and expose adulterers being what the newpapers on Sunday called 'intimate'.

Comfortable, secure, cosy?

■ ■ ■

What is most striking about earlier periods in Australian history—say the 1830s to the 1880s—is the sense of openness and optimism the place generated, in spite of droughts, economic slumps like the one that shook the country in the early 1840s, or the disappointing discovery that the continent had no great inland river system like that in the United States.

As early as 1810, Lachlan Macquarie, newly arrived as Governor of NSW, speaks in a letter to his brother of the 'flourishing condition' in which he found the colony. 'Indeed the whole country' he writes, 'is much more advanced in every kind of improvement than I could have supposed possible in the time it has been settled.' He did not add that this was the more remarkable because for all but three or four years of those years Britain had been engaged in a major Continental war with Napoleon and the French.

Peter Cunningham, in 1828, writes of 'gentlemen foreigners, tempted by the fineness of our country and climate to take up permanent abode among us. Frenchmen, Spaniards, Germans ... all add to the variety of language current among us ... In the streets of Sydney, too, may often be seen groups of natives of the numerous South Sea Islands with which we trade ... a considerable proportion of the Othesians and New Zealanders are employed as sailors in the vessels that frequent our ports.' This reminds us that Sydney at this time was still mainly a seaport, and that Australia was still a place open to nationalities other than the British.

Cunningham also remarks on how a passion for the outdoors in all classes of Australians already marks them as quite different from Englishmen. 'Young men,' he writes, 'think no more of swimming out a mile or more, and back, than a stranger would of taking a walk the same distance'—although the great Victorian respectability, which was introduced here two decades before its time by the Macquaries, and in some ways never receded, soon decreed that mixed bathing was unacceptable, and for the sake of decency restricted all bathing to the hours before six in the morning and after six at night.

Australians in those days still thought of themselves for the most part as extraterritorial Britishers, but physically and in attitude they were already different. They enjoyed better living and working conditions than their British counterparts; were, like the Scots, better educated; and saw themselves as having better prospects.

By 1870 Australia was importing one third of all books printed in Great Britain; we were already a nation of voracious readers, and not only of pulp fiction. As Michael Cannon[1] shows from library records in Victoria, the average borrower from the Sandhurst Mechanics Institute read 40 books a year, 10 of them history or biography or political economy.

Sydney and Melbourne had a lively theatrical life: vaudeville, melodrama, the dramatisation of popular novels like *East Lynne* or the *Three Musketeers* or *A Tale of Two Cities*, but also of such local works as *For the Term of His Natural Life* and *Robbery Under*

Arms—the same fare that was available in English and American cities.[2]

German immigrants (Germans were, until the First World War, our largest non-British group; at the time of separation, one in ten Queenslanders was German speaking) introduced musical clubs—Liedertafel[3]—to all the capital cities and to dozens of smaller towns all over the country, importing their own conductors and performing locally composed pieces.

The Lyster Opera Company from San Francisco gave 1459 performances between 1861 and 1868. *Faust*, for example, was presented just six months after its London premiere.[4]

The truth is that Sydney and Melbourne, in the 1860s and 1870s, saw themselves not as colonial cities—Calcutta and Bombay were that—but as great provincial centres, standing in the same relationship to London as Leeds or Manchester or Dublin, and in some ways doing better than those places, and better as well than Washington or Saint Louis.

An English visitor, Henry Cornish, whose *Under the Southern Cross* is one of the classic accounts of nineteenth-century Australia, found Sydney in 1870 'not at all the dull second-rate English town of my expectations'. Archibald Michie, a member of the Victorian Legislative Assembly and author of *Readings in Melbourne*, writing of the southern capital in the 1860s when it was larger than Sydney by 45,000 people, speaks of it as 'a great city, as comfortable, as elegant, as luxurious (it is hardly an exaggeration to say it) as any place out of London or Paris'. When young Australians of talent went overseas they were not fleeing a cultural desert. They were doing what ambitious young people from Manchester did, or Boston or New York: taking their genius, if they had one, to where it could be put to the test. And London, even for Australians, was not always the Mecca. They were provincial, not chauvinistic. For painters it was Paris, where John Peter Russell and Hugh Ramsay went to study; while for musicians like the young Henry Handel Richardson, it was Leipzig, as it was also for the composer Alfred Hill, who played in the Gewandhaus Orchestra at the first performance of the Brahms Fourth.

So what went wrong? Where did it all go, that early self confidence and ebullience, that bouncy belief of the clever lad from the provinces, the seventh son, in the world's infinite possibilities and his own abounding good luck?

Some of it disappeared into the sand with those inland rivers; much more in the downward turn of the economy that began in the 1890s and lasted right up to the Second World War. More again was drained away in the horrors of the trenches, in the 60,000 deaths in a population of less than four million, that robbed the country of so much vitality and talent, struck at the heart of the country towns, and left so many women for the rest of their lives without men. The big houses of my Brisbane childhood, the old patrician houses, were inhabited by lone women, the widows and sisters and fiancées of those who had been killed, and whose names were everywhere: on the honour boards at school, on war memorials in suburban parks, in the lists of employees who had served and been killed at the post office and at railway stations and in banks. It was a psychic blow from which the country in some ways never recovered, and which it suffered, for the most part, in silence.

Added to this was the long agony in the 1920s and 1930s of the soldiers' farms, where men who had survived the trenches and taken up what turned out to be marginal farming land found how harsh the land could be, and how little reward they had received for their years of sacrifice. Then, when the Great Depression struck, the bitter lesson that however hard you worked, however self-reliant and resilient you might be, however you clung to the bushman's code, the digger code, of mateship and stoicism and hard-won independence, your life was not in your own hands. The country was at the mercy of outside forces, overseas banks, and market trends that neither you nor the government, it seemed, could control.

Add again the shock of discovering, as was brought

home to Australians again and again in the new century, that loyalty to empire did not necessarily assure you a special place in the priorities of the British Government. Even more alarming, that the wholeness of the society you thought you lived in was an illusion; that Germans, your good, hardworking neighbours, were really the enemy within—or so it appeared—and then, when things settled again, the shameful discovery, or recollection, of how those old friends and neighbours had been treated: the attacks against them in the streets; the law that had prevented them from hiding the disloyalty of their origins by changing their names; the deportation of those who had been interned, and with them their Australian wives and children. So what *was* it to be an Australian? What did it mean to be loyal—to the nation, to your own people? Who could you trust?

Involvement for the first time in a total war had changed things. That was what it was all about. And they could not be changed back.

Emergency restrictions that had been imposed under the extraordinary conditions of war, on pub hours for instance, the famous six o'clock closing, tended to establish themselves, become permanent. Then there was the setting up of a counter-espionage bureau in 1917, an internal spy system to keep a watch on aliens and dissidents and other wartime undesirables, and which, in the decades after the war, became the agency of a growing paranoia about the presence among us of un-Australian elements, whose aim was the destruction of everything we stood for. And the emergence, as a reaction to the presence of Wobblies, anarchists and local Communists inspired by the Russian revolution, of secret armies, mostly of ex-diggers, the White Army, the Old Guard, the New Guard, who were ready if necessary to seize power and set up their own version of Australianness and order. Then, in 1942 came the final blow, the fall of Singapore, and the end of the old belief that we might be left to make our own life here away from interference by a larger world. Thirty thousand of our men were marched into captivity in darkest Asia. It was the fulfilment at last of what had been from the beginning our great nightmare, that those borders that nature itself seemed to have established with just us in mind might not hold. Two hundred and forty-three dead in a single raid on Darwin. Two weeks later, seventy-three more at Broome. Nineteen dead in the midget submarine raid on Sydney. The Americans arrived to protect us from invasion, and some of our saviours, despite our protests to the United States government, turned out to be black. After 1928, black jazz musicians had been banned from entering Australia on the grounds that they were a moral threat to our women. When the American government insisted that blacks must be included in their forces here, we insisted in turn that they should be used only in Queensland and must not be landed either in Sydney or Melbourne.[5]

■ ■ ■

In the dark days after Singapore, Australia, which had put so much faith in the goodwill of the British and the power of the British Fleet, was mocked in Nazi radio broadcasts as 'the Orphan in the Pacific'.[6]

Once again we had been too trusting. Or—another temptation of living on an island—too sleepily closed off in our own little world to see how completely the world around us had moved on.

Through most of the 1920s and 1930s we seem to have been too stunned to take any sort of initiative. It had taken us 11 years to ratify the Statute of Westminster which recognised us as an autonomous nation, and we were 13 years behind Canada, and 11 behind South Africa in having our own, rather than British representatives overseas—even in Washington. We drew in behind our ocean wall and sulked. We turned our back on everything foreign or new or contemporary.

One or two of our painters, Margaret Preston and Grace Cossington Smith, for example, who had studied outside the country, did work that was modernist, and Kenneth Slessor might be called a modernist poet;

but this was rare. Most of our writers were still devoted to bush realism and later to socialist realism. Even Nettie Palmer, the most internationally aware of our literary critics, was anti-modernist. So were Stewart and Hope and McAuley. A. D. Hope, in one of his most frequently quoted poems, speaks from the very heart of educated Australian philistinism, of 'the chatter of cultured apes, which is called civilization over there'.[7] Who are these cultured apes, one wonders, who have failed to pass the test of civilisation as we Australians understand it? Wittgenstein, Benedetto Croce, Walter Benjamin, Jung, Ortega y Gasset, Simone Weil, Thomas Mann?

A fair indication of the cultural climate of the 1930s can be seen in the response of local experts to the *Herald* art show of 1939, when Australians first had the chance to see paintings by Picasso, Braque, Matisse and other twentieth-century masters.

For Lionel Lindsay, as for the Nazis, the School of Paris was a 'Jewish conspiracy'. Australia, until now undefiled, was, he tells us, 'threatened by the same aliens, the same corrupting influences that undermined French art'. Explaining why the Victorian gallery would not be buying any of the show's works, the director, James MacDonald, told journalists: 'The great majority of the work called "modern" is the product of degenerates and perverts … As the owner of a great Van Dyck, if we take a stand by refusing to pollute our gallery with this filth, we shall render a service to art.'

This is the same J. MacDonald who believed that if we kept ourselves pure, and free of taint from inferior types like Asians and southern Europeans, we might become 'the elect of the world, the thoroughbred Aryans in all their nobility'.[8]

One sees here, in the language as well as the attitudes, why Australia did not benefit from the exodus of European intellectuals in the mid to late 1930s that created, in America, the new intellectual disciplines that would be so influential for the rest of the century. In this sense, too, Australia was closed. Between 1936 and 1940 just 3828 migrants landed on our shores.

James McAuley's great phrase, 'the faint sterility that disheartens and derides',[9] seems to me to express most clearly the mood of Australia in the 1920s and 1930s, and it was still there, along with all the old terrors of life both within and without, and with tea and butter and petrol rationing, at the beginning of the 1950s.

And then?

Sheer panic at our lack of numbers, at a birthrate that had fallen 25 per cent since 1870, made the Labor government, after the war, embark on an ambitious migrant program.

No Asians, of course. As Minister for Immigration Arthur Calwell is reported to have put it in 1947:

'Two Wongs do not make a White', and our agents were to give preference in the DP camps to people with fair hair and blue eyes. But the important thing was, we were open to the world again.

These people would bring more than themselves. They would bring the world and new ways of looking at it; new models of what an Australian might be, might care for, aspire to, sell his soul for; new notions, whatever the demands of local conformity, of how one might want to live one's life.

But the real source of change was another newcomer that we let in at last in 1956, and not just into the country but into our homes. Television. That little black box was also a mirror. Looking into it we would see our real faces at last, and how many and various we were: women who argued and had opinions; blacks, homosexuals, young people whose tastes and ideas were different from those of their elders.

Television taught us to look and listen. It gave us a new image of ourselves and a new version of local culture—a popular, commercial culture that we too, these days, export to the world. Most of all, it got us to open up and *talk*. To break the great Australian silence. To break out of a disabling tradition of close-lipped devotion to the unspoken, the inexpressible, that had kept so much pain—and so much love, too, one suspects—unacknowledged because it could not find words.

■　■　■

One of the ways in which we deal with the randomness of what happens to us is by seeing it as a story, imposing on it the *shape* of story. Perhaps this is why folk tales and fairy tales mean so much to us. They offer a range of story-shapes—Cinderella, Sleeping Beauty, Hansel and Gretel, Beauty and The Beast, Puss-in-Boots, the Joseph story—that are models for turning the muddle of living from one day to the next into something with a middle and an end. Novels do the same: picaresque novels like *Don Quixote*; the growing-older-and-wiser novel the Germans call a *Bildungsroman*; love stories like *Jane Eyre*; the novel of the divided self like *Dr Jekyll and Mr Hyde*; novels of self-reliance and salvation through work like *Robinson Crusoe*. And national myths, too, follow these prototype narratives. That is why the representation of us as the 'Orphan in the Pacific' was so cruel.

Two elements are worth noting here: our tendency to see ourselves as childlike, forever in the process of growing up or coming of age, and the self-pitying sense of being unloved and abandoned by a bad stepmother, in a place far from home.

Anxiety about where we are, what we are to be, an endless fussing and fretting over identity, has been with us now for more than a century. Perhaps it is time we discovered a new shape for the story we have been telling ourselves.

Identity can be experienced in two ways. Either as a confident *being-in-the-world* or as anxiety about *our-place-in-the-world*; as something we live for ourselves, or as something that demands for its confirmation the approval of others.

Perhaps it is time to stop asking what our Asian neighbours will think of us, or the Americans or the British, and try living free of all watchers but our own better and freer and more adventurous selves.

6

A Spirit of Play

One of the things we seem to find difficult is to see our history—all that happened and was done here—as a continuity, a whole. And this for more than the usual reasons: that historians differ in their reading of what happened and why—on the reasons, for example, for the founding of the colony—or because we have, each one of us, an emotional or ideological investment in such questions as why the Aborigines died out so quickly after we came, whether by accident through the spreading of disease or through deliberate extermination, and the extent to which the way we acted towards them may have departed from British Government policy. Disagreements of this sort are common to historians everywhere. Our problem is different. It is one of selective memory. We remember the bits that speak well of us, the freedoms we have achieved, the good life we have created for so many here; the dark bits we suppress.

The truth is that our history has not been one of unbroken progress, either materially or socially. It has been a continuous shifting back and forth: between periods of economic boom and long periods of depression; between a confident openness to the world, and to our own capacity for experiment, and a cautious drawing in behind defensive walls; between a brave inclusiveness and a panicky need to make distinctions and exclude. But it *is* a continuity, and we need to take it whole.

What each of us takes on, at whatever point we enter it, is the *whole* of what happened here, since it is the whole of our history that has created what now surrounds and sustains us. We cannot disassociate ourselves from the past by saying we were not present. It is present in us. And we must resist the attractive notion that the past is, as they say, another country. It is not. It is this country before the necessities of a changing world changed it.

As for the wish to return to the past in the belief

that it was somehow simpler and more truly 'Australian' because less various—all one can say is, there *are* no simplicities, there never were. Life is always more complex than the means we have for dealing with it. It always has been. We change, but not fast enough. That's the way things are. As for our Australianness, that has always been a matter of argument, of experiment. What is extraordinary in the society we have developed here is the rapidity of the changes it has undergone, and we feel this all the more when we see them tumbling in, one upon the other, within the span of our own lives.

Some of these changes are changes of attitude, of the way we see the world; others, more radically, are changes in the way we see ourselves.

■   ■   ■

When Europeans first came to this continent they settled in the cooler, more temperate parts of it. This was where they could reproduce to some extent the world they had left, but it was also because they saw themselves as cool-climate people. The wisdom, 50 years ago, was that white men would never live and work in the north.

Well, we seem to have re-invented ourselves in these last years as warm-climate people. Not only do we live quite comfortably in the north, it is where a great many of us prefer to live. If present population trends are anything to go by, a large part of our population in the next century will have moved into the tropics, and Queensland, our fastest growing state, will be our local California.

This is a change of a peculiar kind. A change in the way we define ourselves and our relationship to the world that is also a new way of experiencing our own bodies. And the second change I have in mind is related to this. It is the change in the living habits of Australians that we can observe any night of the week in Lygon Street in Melbourne, in Rundle Street, Adelaide, in various parts of Sydney: people eating out on the pavement under the stars in a style we recognise immediately as loosely Mediterranean, a style that has become almost universal in these last years, but which fits better here than it does in Toronto or Stockholm.

It seems to me to be the discovery of a style at last that also fits the kind of people we have now become, and that fits the climate and the scene. But the attitudes it expresses, also loosely Mediterranean, make the sharpest imaginable contrast with the way we were even two decades ago, the way, in that far-off time, that we saw life and the possibilities of living.

Look at these diners. Look at what they are eating and drinking: at the little dishes of olive oil for dipping their bread, the grilled octopus, the rocket, the tagines and skordalia, the wine. Look at the eye for style—for local style—with which they are dressed and their easy acceptance of the body, their tendency to dress it up, strip it, show it off. Consider what all this suggests of a place where play seems natural, and pleasure a part of what living is for; then consider how far these ordinary Australians have come from that old distrust of the body and its pleasures that might have seemed bred in the bone in the Australians we were even 30 years ago. These people have changed, not just their minds but their psyches, and have discovered along the way a new body. They have slipped so quickly and so easily into this other style of being that they might have been living this way, deep in a tradition of physical ease, a comfortable accommodation between soul and body, for as long as grapes have grown on vines or olives on trees.

But half a lifetime ago, in the 1950s, olive oil was still a medicine and spaghetti came in tins. Eating out for most Australians was steak and chips at a Greek café if you were on the road, or the occasional Chinese meal. We ate at home, and we ate pretty much what our grandparents had eaten, even those of us whose grandparents came from elsewhere: lamb chops, Irish stew, a roast on Sundays. It would have seemed ludicrous to take food seriously—to write about it in the newspaper, for example—or to believe that what we ate might constitute a 'cuisine', something new and original, a product of art as well as necessity, an expression, in the same way that 'Waltzing Matilda' or 'Shearing the Rams' might be, of a national style and of the local spirit at play.

As for those other changes—of attitude, ways of seeing ourselves in relation to one another and to the world—I shall mention only two. Both were once so deeply embedded in all our ways of thinking here they might have seemed essential to what we were. We could scarcely have imagined an Australia without them.

The first was that belief in racial superiority and exclusiveness that went under the name of the White Australia Policy, but was really, until the end of the Second World War, an exclusively British policy. As the *Bulletin* put it with its usual brutal candour: 'Australia for the Australians—the cheap Chinese, the cheap Nigger, and the cheap European pauper to be absolutely excluded'.

These sentiments, this sort of language, which was common to the *Bulletin* and to later popular papers like *Smith's Weekly* right up to the early 1950s, expressed the policy of *all* political parties, left and right, and seemed not only acceptable but unremarkable. Both the attitudes and the language were inextricably tied in with our concept of nationhood. Or so it seemed. Yet the White Australia policy, when it disappeared in the 1960s, did so almost without argument. This great tenet of the Australian dream, of a single superior race on the continent, had grown so weak and theoretical by the 1960s that it simply vanished as if it had never been, and, despite recent rumblings, seems to me to show no signs of revival.

So, too, amazingly, did what had been from the beginning the strongest of all divisions among us, the sectarian division between Protestants and Catholics.

When I was growing up in Brisbane, in the late 1930s and early 1940s, Catholic and Protestant Australians lived separate lives. They might have been living in separate countries. The division between them, the separation, the hostility, was part of the very fabric of living; so essential to life here, so old and deeply rooted, as to seem immemorial and impossible to change.

Catholics and Protestants went to separate schools and learned different versions of history. Secondary students even went to different dancing classes, and when they left school they played football with different clubs, joined different lodges (the Order of Ancient Buffaloes or the Oddfellows if they were Protestant, the Hibernians if they were Catholic), and debutantes came out at different balls. People knew by instinct, at first meeting, by all sorts of tell-tale habits of speech and attitude, who belonged to one group and who to another, just as they knew which corner shops or department stores they should patronise. And these divisions functioned institutionally as well as at street level. Catholics worked in some areas of the Public Service, Protestants in others. In Queensland, the Labor Party was Catholic; Protestants were Liberals. In the two great referenda over conscription, in 1916 and 1917, the country divided not on party but on sectarian lines—Protestants for, Catholics against—although in the end the 'no's' won; and one should add that serving soldiers were as likely to be Catholic as not.

Part of the bitterness behind all this was that Catholics were almost exclusively Irish, so that the division had an ethnic and historical element as well as a religious one. It was a continuation on new ground of the history of Ireland itself, based on ancient resistance to English invasion and tyranny, and on the English side on fear of Irish subversion and a deep-rooted contempt for Irish superstition and disorderliness. All this created its own mythology. The suggestion, for instance, that bushranging in Australia was a new version of Irish rebellion. It is true that most of the best-known bushrangers, real and imaginary, have Irish names, but as so often, what is told and strongly felt is not necessarily what is true to fact. The Kelly gang was Irish, but so were Kennedy, Scanlon and Lonigan, the three troopers they killed at Stringybark Creek. So were the police who hunted them. Then, too, to be

Irish here did not always mean that you had Irish forebears.

My father's people were Melkites, Greek Catholics who recognise the authority of the Pope. Since there was no Melkite church in Brisbane when they arrived there in the 1880s (or anywhere else in Australia for that matter), my father and his six brothers and sisters went to the local Catholic church, St Mary's, and were sent to school with the nuns. Despite their name and background, they grew up as Irish as any Donohue or O'Flynn, taking on with the religion all the peculiar forms of Irish Catholicism, its pietism, its prudery, its superstitions and prejudice. To be Catholic in Australia in those days was to be Irish, wherever you came from.

And what exactly was at stake in all this? To a Protestant militant like John Dunmore Lang, the continent itself.

For Irish Catholics in Australia, Protestants were not only in the ascendance as they had been At Home, but in the majority. For Protestants the fear was that this happy condition might one day be reversed; that they might wake up one morning and find they had been outnumbered and that this great continent had fallen overnight to Rome and to Maridolatory.

That Catholics did become the majority at last in the late 1980s, and nobody noticed, is a mark of how large the change has been. Young people today not only feel none of the old hostility. For the most part they have never even heard of it. And this is not only because of the increasing secularity of our society, although that too is part of it. It is because these differences no longer matter. The whole sorry business is worth recalling now for only one reason, and it is this. If Australia is basically, as I believe it is, a tolerant place, that tolerance was hammered out painfully and over nearly a 150 years in the long process by which Catholics and Protestants, the Irish and the rest, turned away from 'history' and learned to live with one another in a way that, for all its bitterness of distrust and resentment, was never murderous as it had been elsewhere, even in times of the greatest stress: during the Easter uprising of 1916, for example, and the Irish Civil War of the early 1920s; or, before that, during the Home Rule controversy of the 1880s, or before that again, in 1868, when a suspected Fenian named O'Farrell tried to assassinate the visiting Alfred, Duke of Edinburgh at Clontarf.

This rejection of the move from hostility to murder is important. The smell of blood is not easily forgotten. The stain of it is hard to eradicate and the names of the dead are always there to be reiterated and to become the source of a new round of violence.

Something in the tone of Australian society has been unwelcoming of extremes, and if this makes for a certain lack of passion, a lack of the swagger and high rhetoric that begins as theatre and ends as terrorism and war, it has also *saved* us from something. In contrast to some other mixed societies, like Ireland itself, central Europe in the 1930s, and, most recently, Lebanon and Bosnia, some final sanction has always operated here against the negation of that deep psychological work that over something like six millennia has made it possible for us to live with strangers and, however different they might be from ourselves, make neighbours of them.

And isn't this, finally, what holds civilised societies together? The capacity to make a distinction between what belongs, in the way of loyalty, to clan or sect or family, and what to the demands of neighbourliness; what belongs to our individual and personal lives and what we owe to *res publica* or Commonwealth, the life we share with others, even those who may differ from us in the most fundamental way—skin colour and ethnicity, religious and political affiliation, customary habits. It is the capacity to make and honour these distinctions, out of a common concern for the right we have, each one of us, to pursue our own interests, that is essential to the life of cities, and beyond that, to their more precarious extension as states.

On the whole, we have done well in this. Not only in creating a society in which these distinctions *are* recognised and honoured, but in creating a tone that those who come here from places where they are not, quickly learn to value and accept. There is something to be said for mildness. It leaves people the breathing space, and the energy, to get on with more important things. As George Nadel[1] puts it in speaking of the fight for decent working conditions in Australia: 'The fact that it appeared within reach of everyone made democratic experiment safe, and the working classes were satisfied to secure their share by enjoying a greater return for less labour rather than by political radicalism.' That is, there have been no revolutions in Australia, no blood, at least in this instance, has stained the wattle.

The world these days is global. Australians have not escaped the pressures of the complex present; we will not escape the pressures of an even more complex future. In daring to become a diverse and multi-ethnic society, an open experiment, we run more risk perhaps than most places of breaking up, of fragmenting. But we have faced danger before. What saved us on those earlier occasions was neighbourliness, the saving grace of lightness and good humour, the choice of moderation over the temptation to any form of extreme. These characteristics of our society are still visibly alive in the present; in occasions we take for granted, so much so that we fail sometimes to see how rare they are.

Consider the atmosphere in which election days are celebrated here. The spirit of Holiday hovers over our election boxes. As the guardian angel of our democracy, it seems preferable, and might even be more reliable, than the three or four bored paratroopers who descend to protect the ballot-boxes in even the smallest village in a place as politically sophisticated as Italy. Voting for us is a family occasion, a duty fulfilled, as often as not, on the way to the beach, so that children, early, get a sense of it as an obligation but a light one, a duty casually undertaken. And it can seem casual. But the fact that voters so seldom spoil their vote, either deliberately or by accident, in a place where voting is compulsory and voting procedures are often extremely complicated, speaks for an electorate that has taken the trouble to inform itself because it believes these things matter, and of a citizenship lightly but seriously assumed.

I ended my first chapter with the description of an audience, a mixed convict and military one, at a performance in 1800 of Shakespeare's *Henry IV Part One.* What I wanted to see in it was a first attempt here at a society in which all sorts of divisions between groups, but also between individuals, might be resolved by the fact that, in becoming an audience, this heterogeneous crowd had also, for the duration of the occasion, become an entity—and perhaps a single occasion, single occasions, is the best we can hope for, and is enough: a recognition that unity is there as a possibility. It does not have to be sustained as long as it is available when we need it to be.

Let me end with another audience, one in which what was promised in that earlier audience seems to me to be marvellously fulfilled, under more complex conditions and on a vastly larger scale.

An audience comes together of its own volition, unlike a rally, for example, where there is always some element of compulsion, if only a moral one of commitment or duty. An audience simply appears, as the 700,000 or so people do who turn out each year for the gay Mardi Gras procession in Sydney. They have no reason for being there other than interest, curiosity, pleasure, and they are an audience, not simply a crowd, an audience that has been created and shaped by the society it is drawn from, and in which the faculty of watching, listening and judging has been sharpened to an extraordinary degree.

What impresses me about this audience is its capacity to read what it is presented with and come up with an appropriate response: to greet extravagant glitter and camp with delight and a degree of humourous mockery; to see that deliberate provocation is best dealt with by a shrug of the shoulders or live-and-let-live indifference, but that a more sober note is being struck when people incapacitated by AIDS are being wheeled past, and that what is called for by the large throng of their nurses and carers is the acknowledgement of service with respectful silence or applause.

No one has trained this audience in its responses:

they come naturally out of what has been picked up from the society itself, they reflect its 'tone'. It is, as an audience, as mysterious in the way it appears and reconstitutes itself for each occasion as any other. No one 20 years ago could have predicted its arrival, but there it is.

As for the actors in this street theatre—could anyone have guessed, back then, that it would be just this group that would call a popular audience into being? Another mystery.

What seems extraordinary here, is that what, until recently, had been a marginal group, mostly invisible, has not only made itself visible but has made the claim as well to be central—that is, as central as any other—and has created that audience for all of us. Open, inclusive, the parade is made up of virtually every strand in our society: the various ethnicities, including Asian and Pacific people and Aborigines; members of the armed forces, the police, and of every other profession, including sex-workers. In being multiple itself, such a parade offers the crowd a reflected image of its own multiplicity, and all within a spirit of carnival, a form of play that includes mockery and self-mockery, glamour and the mockery of glamour, social comment, tragedy and a selfless dedication to others, as if all these things were aspects of the same complex phenomenon—as of course they are. It is called life.

Carnival deals with disorder by making a licensed

place for it, and with the threat of fragmentation by reconstructing community in a spirit of celebratory lightness. It takes on darkness and disruption by embracing them. Forces that might otherwise emerge as violence, it diverts through tolerance and good humour into revelry and sheer fun.

Such carnival occasions have ancient roots. They go back to the pagan world, and to medieval festivals, days of licence, Fools' Days, when the spirit of mockery was let loose and a place found for disorder within the world of order and rule. For all its contemporary glitz and high jinks, our version of Mardi Gras retains much of its ancient significance. As a popular festival it reinforces community. It recovers for us, within the complexities and the divisiveness of modern living, a sense of wholeness. And there is a connection here between the carnival world it celebrates, its vulgarity, its flaunting of the flesh, and that first convict performace of *Henry IV.*

Falstaff, the randy, disreputable anti-hero of that play, is the great embodiment in our literature of the spirit of carnival, the direct descendant of the Vice that larked about at the centre of the old morality plays, and before that of the Lords of Misrule, who presided over medieval Fools' Days. Falstaff, and the disorder he represents, is what has somehow to be included in the world of Rule. 'Banish plump Jack', he tells Prince Hal, 'and banish all the world.'

Falstaff, with his shameless insistence on the flesh, his dirty jokes and phallic shenanigans, is a necessary aspect of what it is to be alive. So is the challenge his non-conformism offers to the coldness and impersonality of the law. Finding a place for Falstaff, acting imaginatively in the spirit of lightness he represents, is the way to wholeness; and wholeness, haleness, as the roots of our language tell us, is health.

Notes

1. The Island

1. Rudyard Kipling, 'Recessional', 1897.
2. Sydney, who as Secretary for the Home Department was responsible for the establishment of the colony, seems to have intended that transported convicts, once they arrived at Botany Bay, should be 'free on the ground'; that is, their sentences, 7 or 14 years or life, were terms of exile, not of bondage. One of the arguments in favour of Botany Bay as the site for the colony was that there were no people there who might put the men and women who were sent there under bond, as they had been, for example, in Virginia. As for labour, the convicts might work for their keep until the colony was established but forced labour had been

declared unconstitutional in 1783, on the grounds that it reduced a man to slavery and no free-born Briton, even a convicted felon, should be put in the same condition as a slave.

Governor Phillip chose to ignore all this. He put his convicts in bond to the Crown and, unless they were pardoned, until the last day of their sentence. There is the pathetic case of William Bradbury who had, it was thought, served his 7 years, partly on The Hulks (those old prison ships anchored in the Thames and off Portsmouth), partly on the voyage out, and who was granted land at Parramatta. But when the Second Fleet arrived with the records, his sentence was found to be for life. Phillip took him back into bondage, and when he protested had him flogged. In despair, Bradbury ran off into the scrub and was never heard of again.

In this business of flogging, too, Phillip's decision was to be fateful. Civil floggings were largely symbolic, their aim to humiliate the victim in front of his peers, not to break him physically. What Phillip did was impose on the civilian convicts the naval practice of flogging by numbers and to the last lash.

These decisions had their severest consequences long after Phillip had left the colony when, at the end of the Napoleonic wars, large numbers of convicts began to arrive at Botany Bay, and the demand for labour in the colony, both for public works and for work on private farms, made bonded labour both useful and profitable. But it is worth noting that one of the privileges allowed to convicts in New South Wales was the retention of their property. A man who could support himself and did not draw food from the Stores could exempt himself from government labour, as James Grant did, for example, in 1804. And once a man had completed his government labour he was free to hire himself out for private work. When the price of labour in the colony rose to 4 and 5 shillings a day, a skilled workman, such as a bricklayer or carpenter, could work for himself and pay another man to do his government work for him. Women from the beginning did no government work at all. As Alan Atkinson puts it in *The Europeans in Australia*, 'In these first years of European settlement (after Phillip's time and up to Macquarie's) even convict men and women who came with no money entered a market as much as they did a penal system.'

3. John Locke, *Second Treatise on Civil Government*, 1690. One of the cornerstones of English political thinking.

4. At the debates held at Putney in 1649, at the end of the English Civil War, the Diggers and Levellers and other pre-communist groups who made up a large part of Parliament's New Model Army argued for the establishment of an egalitarian commonwealth and for universal male suffrage independent of the ownership of land. They were defeated by Cromwell and the other Grandees, and when some of them, the Diggers,

being landless, occupied and began to dig common land, they were driven off in a series of bloody skirmishes. These sects were the organised and articulate nucleus of what Christopher Hill, in his *The World Turned Upside Down*, calls 'masterless men', who in the break-up of the old feudal system constituted a new class, of vagabonds, beggars, itinerant labourers, and the urban poor. As early as 1594 we hear of them being rounded up and transported to Ireland as a way of relieving the kingdom of its 'superfluous people'—Ireland, in this way, preceding Virginia and, later, New South Wales as repositories of the unwanted and refractory.

We see something of the ideas that were common among utopian radicals in the early seventeenth century from Gonzalo's speech in *The Tempest*:

> I' the commonwealth I would by contraries
> Execute all things; for no kind of traffic
> Would I admit; no name of magistrate;
> Letters should be unknown; riches, poverty,
> And use of service, none; contract, succession,
> Bourn, bound of land, tilth, vineyard, none;
> No use of metal, corn, or wine, or oil,
> No occupation; all men idle, all;
> And all women too, but innocent and pure;
> No sovereignty ...

This was religious as well as a political wisdom, in

which the ownership of property, the use, through monopoly, of common goods, the rule of one man over another as king or bishop or magistrate, the use of one man's service in another's interest, was a result of the Fall, and Abel's murder at the hands of Cain the origin of one 'brother's' ascendancy over another in a fallen world.

5. When Worgan left the colony, his piano passed into the hands of Elizabeth Macarthur. It still exists. See *The Oxford Companion to Australian Music.*

6. One of the privileges of convicted felons in New South Wales was that all charges by or against them had to be heard by a magistrate. By a legal fiction they appeared not as felons but under their old designation, as labourer or hedger or haberdasher, and had the right as well to use their own slang, their thieves cant or 'kiddy' language, which the court, if necessary, translated.

2. A Complex Fate

1. Letter, 1872, quoted in *Letters of Henry James,* vol. 1 (ed. Percy Lubbock).

2. Judith Wright in 'Poetry until 1920' in *The Literature of Australia* (ed. Geoffrey Dutton).

3. ibid.

4. This phrase I owe to Aboriginal elder and teacher Mary Graham, whose thinking is a model of the way indigenous and non-indigenous approaches to the world can be reconciled and draw strength from one another

in an understanding larger than might be possible to either separately.

3. Landscapes

1. The Polish poet Zbigniew Herbert gives a brilliant account of the tulip craze in 'The Bitter Smell of Tulips', a 'story of human folly' in *Still Life with a Bridle*. It is also the subject, of course, of Alexandre Dumas' *Le Tulip Noire.*

2. *Oral Poetry* (ed. Ruth Finnegan).

3. Eric Rolls, 'The Nature of Australia' in *Ecology and Empire* (eds Tom Griffiths and Libby Robin).

4. ibid.

5. Eric Rolls, 'Voicing the Land' in *Land and Identity* (eds Jennifer McDonnell and Michael Deves).

6. English iconoclasm came in three waves. The first, at the time of the dissolution of the monasteries under Henry VIII, was political, an official vandalism; the others, under Elizabeth I and during the Civil War, were outbreaks of popular fanaticism. The earlier of the two led to the maiming of the sculptural figures on the west front of Wells Cathedral, probably the finest in England, and in the Lady Chapel at Ely, which, in being dedicated to the Virgin, was an especial affront to Protestant sensibilities. The later wave took place mainly in East Anglia. Matthew Hopkins, the self-styled Witchfinder General, seems to have combined witch-finding with smashing stained glass in all the towns and

villages of Essex, Sussex, Huntingdonshire, and his native Norfolk. He was responsible for the torture and execution of more than 100 men and women in these counties, but eventually fell victim to his own methods. Examined and found to be a witch, he was hanged in August 1647. He makes a brief appearance in Samuel Butler's seventeenth-century mock-heroic epic, *Hudibras*, and was the subject, in 1969, of a 'period horror film' starring Vincent Price.

4. Monuments to Time

1. David Malouf, *12 Edmonstone Street*.
2. Palladianism was first introduced into England by Inigo Jones, whose Banqueting Hall at Westminster and the Queen's House at Greenwich (designed 1616 and completed just before the Civil War) show Palladio's influence. It is significant that Jones was best-known as a theatre designer working on court masques in collaboration with Ben Jonson (cf. Nikolaus Pevsner, *An Outline of European Architecture*).
3. Alexander Pope, 'Essay on Burlington' in *Moral Essays*.
4. John James Clark was born in Liverpool in 1838. He studied architecture at the Collegiate Institute there, migrated to Australia in 1853, and is credited in 1857, at the age of nineteen, with the design of Melbourne's Treasury Building, which is considered to have 'the finest public building exterior' in Australia. He won competitions for town halls in Orange in New South

Wales and at Waverley in Sydney, and in 1883 was appointed Queensland Colonial Architect, succeeding F. D. A. Stanley, builder of Brisbane's Palladian Post Office and the National Bank. The Queensland Treasury is Clark's best-known Brisbane building and the city's finest nineteenth-century monument.

5. The Orphan in the Pacific

1. Michael Cannon, *The Roaring Years*.
2. Eric Irvin, *A Dictionary of Australian Theatre*.
3. These Liedertafels were men's singing clubs, though some of them also had sister clubs for women (cf. *The Oxford Companion to Australian Music*). They performed in German but for a wider audience. Some of them ceased to exist during the First World War; others simply changed their names. They form an important strand in our musical history, very different in style from the one that comes down to us through the English choral tradition and the Welsh eisteddfod.
4. Stendhal in his *Life of Rossini* remarks that it is 'High Society'—he uses the English formulation—'which outside Italy is the only social class which cultivates music at all'. This seems not to have been true in Australia, where opera, as in Italy, was popular with all classes, as it was also in America. The Lyster operas drew a good number of single young men, including clerks and artisans. They bought tickets to the stalls where prostitutes also went, as they did to

the bar close by. (The bar at the Theatre Royal, because of the large number of prostitutes it attracted, was known as the 'Saddling Paddock'.) When wowserism in the 1870s had the bars removed from theatres, and prohibited single women entrance, this audience was largely lost.

It is difficult to assess the quality of these opera performances. Harold Love, in *The Golden Age of Australian Opera*, quotes an Australian visitor to Florence who found the performances there poor in comparison to what he was used to at home. Love thinks he was exaggerating; but Verdi, in recalling the rehearsal of *Nabucco* at which he first heard 'I pensieri', spoke of the Chorus singing 'as badly as usual', and the *Memoires* of Berlioz are a record of the poorness of contemporary performances in France.

5. Brisbane, under American 'occupation', became a segregated city: blacks were not permitted to cross the river. Well out of sight of southern eyes they built Garbutt Airfield at Townsville, but the streets of South Brisbane, when I was growing up, were full of them.
6. In Robert Lacour-Gayet, *A Concise History of Australia*.
7. A. D. Hope, 'Australia' in *Poems*.
8. Humphrey McQueen, *The Black Swans of Trespass*.
9. James McAuley, 'Envoi' in *Under Aldebaran*.

6. A Sense of Play
1. G. Nadel, *Australian Colonial Culture*.

Bibliography

Atkinson, Alan, *The Europeans in Australia*, Oxford University Press, Melbourne, 1997.

Bebbington, Warren (ed.), *The Oxford Companion to Australian Music*, Oxford University Press, Melbourne, 1997.

Blainey, Geoffrey, *The Tyranny of Distance*, Sun Books, Melbourne, 1966.

Broadbent, James and Joy Hughes (eds), *The Age of Macquarie*, Melbourne University Press, Melbourne, 1992.

Cannon, Michael, *The Roaring Years*, Thomas Nelson, Melbourne, 1992.

Clark, C. M. H., *A History of Australia* (six volumes), Melbourne University Press, Melbourne, 1962–87.

Day, David, *Claiming a Continent,* Angus & Robertson, Sydney, 1996.

Dutton, Geoffrey (ed.), *The Literature of Australia,* Penguin, Melbourne, 1966.

Finnegan, Ruth (ed.), *Oral Poetry,* University of Indiana Press, Bloomington, 1978.

Flannery, Tim, *The Future Eaters,* Reed, Melbourne, 1994.

Frost, Alan, *Botany Bay Mirages,* Melbourne University Press, Melbourne, 1994.

Griffiths, Tom and Robin, Libby (eds), *Ecology and Empire,* Melbourne University Press, Melbourne, 1997.

Herbert, Zbigniew, *Still Life with Bridle,* Jonathan Cape, London, 1993.

Hill, Christopher, *The World Turned Upside Down,* Penguin, London, 1991.

Irvin, Eric (ed.), *A Dictionary of Australian Theatre 1788–1914,* Hale and Iremonger, Sydney, 1985.

Lacour-Gayet, Robert, *A Concise History of Australia,* Penguin, Melbourne, 1974.

Love, Harold, *The Golden Age of Australian Opera,* Currency Press, Sydney, 1998.

McDonnell, Jennifer and Deves, Michael (eds), *Land and Identity,* ASAL, Armidale, 1997.

Macintyre, Stuart, *Oxford History of Australia (Vol. IV),* Oxford University Press, Melbourne, 1986.

McQueen, Humphrey, *A New Britannia,* Penguin, Melbourne, 1986.

McQueen, Humphrey, *The Black Swans of Trespass,*
Sydney Alternative Publishers, Sydney, 1979.

Malouf, David, *12 Edmonstone Street,* Penguin,
Melbourne, 1986.

Nadel, G., *Australian Colonial Culture,* Harvard
University Press, Cambridge, Mass., 1957.

O'Farrell, Patrick, *The Irish in Australia,* NSW University
Press, Sydney, 1986.

Pevsner, Nikolaus, *An Outline of European Architecture,*
Penguin, New York, 1990.

Rolls, Eric, *A Million Wild Acres,* Thomas Nelson,
Melbourne, 1981.

Watson, Donald and McKay, Judith, *Queensland
Architects of the Nineteenth Century,* Queensland
Museum Publication, Brisbane, 1994.

White, Richard, *Inventing Australia,* Allen & Unwin,
Sydney, 1980.